Praise for *Social Media Geek-to-Geek*

"Geeks have a unique culture and live by different rules—so, if you want to reach them successfully through social media, you need this book. Rick and Kathy tapped their real-world tested experience to fill this book with advice that you can put to use immediately."
Charlene Li, Author, "Open Leadership" and Founder, Altimeter Group

"Social Media Geek-to-Geek is a great resource for technologists who use social media to communicate and share real-time information. In our business environment, where transparency and relevancy rules, it's the perfect time to equip geeks alike to join the conversation and have fun!"
Michael Brito, VP, Social Media, Edelman Digital

"We've certainly seen a level of mistrust among the hard-minded business pros—and geeks—who find it hard to believe the hype from all the self-professed social media gurus, ninjas and bandwagoneers. That's why Social Media Geek-to-Geek *is so timely. Talking G2G provides a practical roadmap for an audience who is well-equipped to move their interests forward through social marketing. And with this focused approach, the book also enables what we believe to be one of the most important factors in social media success: Make it your own."*
Jeff Loomis, Chairman + CEO, Loomis Group

"A fresh view, based on up-to-date marketing experience, and particularly welcome at a time when the ground rules are changing so quickly."
Andrew Betts, Technical Sales & Marketing Consultant, Iconda Solutions

A Note from the Publisher

Thank you for your interest in this business series book from Synopsys Press. *Social Media Geek-to-Geek* was born out of our frustration with other social media marketing books and materials, which generally focus on business-to-business (B2B) and business-to-consumer (B2C) marketing. Our executive editor, Rich Goldman, challenged his Synopsys marketing team to find new ways to engage technical customers using social media, coining the phase "Marketing Geek-to-Geek." Authors Rick Jamison and Kathy Schmidt Jamison relate their experiences inventing and rolling out this social media strategy—both what worked and what didn't. In addition, Rick and Kathy have collaborated with other marketing practitioners and geeks (and people who are both) to include their perspectives in this emerging field. Brian Solis, globally recognized as one of the most prominent thought leaders and published authors in new media, contributed the Foreword.

We hope you enjoy the book and look forward to interacting with you through our social media geek-to-geek blog, The Listening Post, at http://www.synopsys.com/blogs/listeningG2G.

To learn more about this Synopsys Press book and the others in both the technical and business series, please visit http://www.synopsys.com/synopsys_press. Additional copies are available online at http://happyabout.com/synopsyspress or at other online and physical bookstores.

Phil Dworsky
Publisher, Synopsys Press
May, 2011

A Note from the Executive Editor

I am a Geek.

Back in the 1970s, I took one of the nation's first high school computer science courses. I instantly knew that computers would be a big part of my life, and this helped direct me to Syracuse University to study computer science, and to my first two jobs at IBM (as an intern) and Texas Instruments. At IBM, I worked on an IC simulator that is still in use today. Years later, when I went back to work with IBMers, I was surprised at the instant standing that my "Geek Cred" gave to me. It was much easier to connect immediately with the Geeks at IBM, and I was more effective for it. For me, this drove home the first principle of G2G: Geeks appreciate and respect other Geeks, and this is the peer group that they want to interact with.

At Texas Instruments, I led a team responsible for ASIC design libraries. This required close interaction with EDA vendors and led me to realize how much I enjoy working with people. I'm blessed in that my current job as vice president of corporate marketing allows me to combine my two passions of being a Geek and working with people.

When I moved into this job in 2009, the nascent field of social media was all the rage. I knew it would be important to incorporate social media into our marketing mix, so I immediately set off to learn about it. I found that in Silicon Valley, I could attend a seminar on the topic any week of the year, and anybody could attend a webinar on the topic any day of the week. But none of these sessions resonated with me—they didn't seem to apply well to our situation at Synopsys.

Eventually, I realized all these seminars were about B2C (Business-to-Consumer) or B2B (Business-to-Business), but our business is quite different from either of these. We're not selling shoes or soda or even electronic products to end consumers. We're not even selling supplies to businesses. Synopsys sells very sophisticated chip design software and solutions to very smart electrical engineers.

Our customers are geeks. And so are we at Synopsys. I realized that we need a different strategy to address our customers, one that would resonate with them, not turn them off. We need an approach that would connect our customers' geeks with our technical information and our own geeks.

Our challenge was to use social media marketing to reach people who don't want to be marketed to and aren't known to be particularly social. This led to coining the term G2G (Geek-to-Geek). I looked around and was surprised to find almost no companies practicing G2G marketing. It was then that I realized that we would have to put forth a pioneering effort.

You can hear more about the development of G2G marketing in my 2010 TEDx talk on the subject (http://www.ted.com/tedx/events/768). Kathy, Rick and my entire staff have my eternal gratitude for sharing my G2G passion and for working to develop it into an excellent success for our customers and ourselves. We feel like we have just started down this path. There are miles and miles of roads ahead of us; but, when we look in the rearview mirror, it's gratifying to see all that we have achieved, and I hope that this book will help you get down that road faster while avoiding some of the many potholes along the way.

Rich Goldman, Executive Editor
VP, corporate marketing & strategic alliances at Synopsys

Social Media Geek-to-Geek

Practical Insights for Technology Marketers

By Rick Jamison and Kathy Schmidt Jamison

Executive Editor Rich Goldman
Cartoons by Rick Jamison
Foreword by Brian Solis

SYNOPSYS®
Press

Mountain View, CA, USA

Rick Jamison and Kathy Schmidt Jamison
Synopsys, Inc.
Mountain View, CA
USA

Library of Congress Control Number: 2011906348
Paperback ISBN: 978-1-61730-007-3 (1-61730-007-1)
eBook ISBN: 978-1-61730-008-0 (1-61730-008-X)

Copyright © 2011 by Synopsys, Inc. All rights reserved.

This work may not be translated or copied in whole or in part without the written permission of Synopsys, Inc. (700 E. Middlefield Road, Mountain View, CA 94043 USA), except for brief excerpts in connection with reviews or scholarly analysis. Use in connection with any form of information storage and retrieval, electronic adaptation, computer software, or by similar or dissimilar methodology now known or hereafter developed is forbidden. The use in this publication of trade names, trademarks, service marks and similar terms, even if they are not identified as such, is not to be taken as an expression of opinion as to whether or not they are subject to proprietary rights.

Published by Synopsys, Inc., Mountain View, CA, USA
http://www.synopsys.com/synopsys_press

Publishing services provided by Happy About®
http://www.happyabout.com

Printed in the United States of America
First Printing: May 2011

Trademarks

Synopsys is a registered trademark of Synopsys, Inc.

All other brands or product names are the property of their respective holders.

Disclaimer

The content included in *Social Media Geek-to-Geek* is the result of the efforts of the authors, Synopsys, Inc. and their contributors. It is presented solely for educational and entertainment purposes. Neither the authors, nor the contributors, nor Synopsys, Inc., nor Happy About, nor any of their affiliates guarantees the accuracy, adequacy or completeness of any information contained herein and neither are they responsible for any errors or omissions, or for the results obtained from the use of such information. THERE ARE NO EXPRESS OR IMPLIED WARRANTIES, INCLUDING, BUT NOT LIMITED TO, WARRANTIES OF MERCHANTABILITY OR FITNESS FOR A PARTICULAR PURPOSE relating to *Social Media Geek-to-Geek*. In no event shall the author, Synopsys, Inc., Happy About, or their affiliates, or any contributor be liable for any indirect, special or consequential damages in connection with the information provided herein.

"Blessed are the learners, for they shall inherit the earth, while the learned find themselves beautifully equipped to deal with a world that no longer exists."

Eric Hoffer, Philosopher

Acknowledgments

This is a fabulous time to be alive, especially if you're a geek—or even if you simply benefit from some of the amazing technologies geeks have dreamed up and made real in recent years.

Social media is literally made possible by geek innovation, including the Internet and every digitally-based form of creative expression that makes social media interesting, engaging, and popular.

We have had the good fortune of being among the early pioneers in our corporate organization to produce, post...and, OK, play...with social media and online content creation in its many manifestations. We will be forever grateful to our managers, colleagues, and other stakeholders at Synopsys for those opportunities, and to Guri Stark in particular for his radical insistence in 2007 that we "just shoot it like YouTube" and for his "cheese merchant in the marketplace" analogy we ~~stole~~ used in the Introduction.

Specific to this book, we wish to thank Buford Barr, Karen Bartleson, Michael Brito, John Chilton, Lou Covey, Tom Diederich, John Donovan, Rich Goldman, Harry "the ASIC Guy" Gries, Jack Harding, Eric Huang, Jamil Kawa, Ed Lee, Godwin Maben, Ron Ploof, Frank Schirrmeister, Guri Stark, and Tom Williams for the geek-focused insights, wisdom, and color they have contributed through the sidebars featured in the pages that follow.

When author, blogger, and social media expert Brian Solis said "yes" to writing the Foreword, words failed us to fully express our appreciation—and evidently they still do. So we simply offer four words for the Foreword: Thank you, Brian Solis.

Finally, we wish to thank Rich Goldman for opening the door that led to the creation of this book, including the idea to focus on the geek-to-geek angle. Thank you Phil Dworsky for your copy editing eagle eyes and expansive questions and comments that led to a better book. Many thanks as well to Karen Bartleson and Ron Ploof for your partnership in developing Synopsys' social media program to its current level of expression, and thank you Herta Schreiner, Jeff Baran, Yvette Huygen, Tao Long, Jesika Gandhi, Hannah Watanabe, Jason Do, and all of the Synopsys bloggers for the learning, implementation, and success we have created together.

Contents

Foreword	Foreword by Brian Solis 1
Introduction	 5
	So, Who's a Geek, Really? 8
	Incoming Marketers 16
	Experienced Communicators 16
	Traditional Marketers 17
	Corporate Managers. 17
Chapter 1	**Stop** **21**
	First Things First. 21
	Who Goes There? 22
	Paint Me a Picture 23
	Dive Deeper 24
	Zoom Back Out. 28
	First-Hand Experience 29
Chapter 2	**Look** **33**
	Look Before You Leap 34
	Best Practices. 36
	Learn from Other People's Mistakes 37
	Apply a Geek Filter. 38
	Shades of Originality 40
Chapter 3	**Synchronize** **45**
	Alignment 45
	Shared Expectations 48
	Trust and Respect 52
	Social Media Policy 52
Chapter 4	**Plan** **59**
	Why Plan? 59
	Land Grab. 60
	The Social Media Sandbox. 64
	Recipe for a Plan 65
	Adaptive Planning. 68

Chapter 5	**Listen**	**71**
	Why Listen?	71
	Systematic Listening	74
	Getting to Know You	76
	What to Do with What You Hear	78
	Beyond Listening	78
	More Reasons to Monitor Your Brand in Cyberspace	79
Chapter 6	**Talk**	**83**
	Why Blog?	84
	Blogging Geek-To-Geek	84
	Corporate Bloggers	85
	Creating a Successful Blogger	88
	Who Owns the Content?	88
	When Bloggers Move On	90
	Creating a Successful Blog	91
	Ideas for Blog Topics	93
	Executive Blogging	96
	Adding Video to a Blog	98
	Take a Test Drive	100
Chapter 7	**Interact**	**105**
	Beyond "All About You"	105
	Style is Everything	108
	Prepare To Banter	109
	Pass the Word	111
	Comments Please?	111
	Geek Tweet	113
	ConnectTweet	114
	Twitter Guidelines	118
	The Art of the Retweet	118
	Online Forums	119
	Knights of the Round Table	120
Chapter 8	**Host**	**123**
	Think Dinner Party	123
	Elevating Others	124
	Guest Bloggers	125
	The Art of the Online Interview	129
	Live Broadcast and Recorded Podcasts	133
	People Who Need People	134

Chapter 9	**Measure**............................ **137**	
	Why Measure?...............................138	
	What to Measure?...........................139	
	Google Analytics.............................142	
	I've Measured—Now What?...................144	
	Analysis-Based Insights......................144	
	The ROI of Social Media 145	
Chapter 10	**Lead**............................... **151**	
	Lead People to Your Content..................152	
	Best Practices in Leading Others to Your Content.153	
	Lead People inside Your Company to Social Media...156	
	Lead the Smart People Outside Your Company to the Smart Ones inside.....................156	
	Lead People into the Unknown................157	
Notes	159	
Authors	About the Authors...........................163	
Synopsys Press	About Synopsys Press.......................165	

Foreword by Brian Solis

Go Your Own Way

When I'm tasked with researching and presenting success stories and best practices in social media, I often ask my clients a bit more about what it is they're specifically seeking. After a bit of interaction, it usually comes down to two words: creative inspiration.

At the moment, social media represents something new, something we understand personally but have yet to comprehend professionally. The unknown is just that, it's undefined. And as such, the paths for exploring new media are uncharted. Rather than find our own way, we seek direction from those who have ventured forth on the roads most travelled. Eventually these expeditions require cartographers to map them, creating a series of charts to what is versus what could be.

Social Media represents change. Change evokes fear, and fear paralyzes us. Yet, all we need is a better understanding of how we got here in order to plan for where we need to go.

I'm sorry to be the one to break it to you, but there is no social media playbook. The only set of instructions that matters are those you write yourself based on the reality of your business and the state of the market. To that end, this book will help you chart your own path.

Everyday people, not businesses, originally embraced social networks. Champions and innovators introduced social media into the organization, from the outside in, because they believed in its ability to reach customers. Through experimentation in day-to-day listening and engagement, social media gained momentum from the bottom-up until it reached a boiling point.

The reality is that there is no IT department for social media. Most of the time, there isn't a Chief Social Officer residing in executive row to help execute against your vision, and the leadership of the organization isn't touting a vision for a more people-focused mission.

Social media is either a playground for the young and restless or it's a cost center. Either way, it's up to us to intimately understand how social media impacts the bottom line and how we can steer experiences, conversations, and action in our direction.

Without engagement, we cannot compete for relevance. Without relevance, we cannot compete.

This is your time to find the answers to your questions. This is your time to become the expert you once sought. Lead the way.

Brian Solis, author of *Engage*
http://www.briansolis.com
@briansolis

Introduction

In the world of geeks, brutal honesty is a cultural imperative. So we begin this book by exposing an unresolved logical tension pair critical to understanding the topic described in the title.

"Social media marketing" is both the topic of this book and a concept that, at best, is highly suspect to geeks and represents everything they distrust about both marketing *and* social media.

There. We've said it. And here's why:

"Social media" is just that: an ever-expanding set of Internet-based platforms, applications, and tools that allow people to create and exchange user-generated content and connect with one another via communities in which they share some basis of common interest. With social media, everyone is a publisher, transparency is king, and the community decides which conversations are of value and which are horse pucky. Given an Internet connection and an electronic device with which to connect, the channels of communication are virtually free of charge and the opportunities to "reach out and touch someone"[1] are endless.

"Marketing," on the other hand, has traditionally lived in the hands of an elite few, mostly paid for by corporations with something to sell. Within corporations, marketing messages are anything but transparent and spontaneous: Just try to get a press release approved without it going 'round and 'round in the business units and back and forth with marketing and other stakeholders, and that's *before* it goes to legal. What is said and who gets to say it is carefully controlled, meticulously vetted, expertly polished, and often quite expensive.

Think about a social media community as a marketplace, and let's say you are a cheese merchant. There are several aspects of that enterprise that *are* under your control: the quality and amount of cheese you make available to your customers, where you set up your cheese stand, how much you charge, and what you say to your customers when they're at your stall. What you cannot control are the number and tone of conversations that take place about your cheese, who participates, when they start and stop, and what's said. In fact, as sad as it is, most of time, the people at the market aren't talking about your cheese at all: They're talking about themselves. So at the outset, a primary goal of corporate participation in social media is to find, create, and all cases, positively influence the conversation.

So when corporations, accustomed to calling the communication shots and controlling every attribute of their brand, decide to join in the wild new create-and-respond freedoms being discovered by their *individual* customers in a virtual marketplace—with the goal to "get their message out"—you have yourself quite a little conundrum called "social media marketing."

So, there's that.

Now, factor in the *geek* element. We'll spend more time in this introduction as well as in future chapters getting our heads around what, exactly, constitutes a geek. Specific to the scope of this book, we'll examine the particular attributes of this demographic that corporations need to understand if they're to stand a chance at having relevant dialogue with their geek communities.

But for now, let's take it at face value that geeks-as-customers share a highly refined sense of smell and can catch the whiff of snake oil and marketing piffle from a million miles of fiber optic cable away. And they don't care for the odor. In addition, geeks value accuracy and logic in their areas of expertise above almost anything else. Layer that into a world described by Andrew Keen in his book, *The Cult of the Amateur*, as being governed by "...the law of digital Darwinism, the survival of the loudest and most opinionated." It's a classic case of oil and water.

Finally, if you work in a company that sells stuff to geeks so those geeks can make other geeky products, chances are pretty good that the people who create your products (i.e., your R & D colleagues) are not just geeks themselves, they're übergeeks. So everything we say here goes double for them. Plus, given that the geeky products they create are highly valuable and vulnerable to piracy, even the non-geeks in your organization (e.g., Legal, Finance, Marketing, PR, HR) are wary of the beast called social media.

Since your geeks create products, tools, and services that are purchased by geek customers who care intensely about safeguarding their own proprietary designs and products, free-flowing dialog in the public domain focused on solving any real-world problems is highly unlikely (or explicitly forbidden by confidentiality policies). Moreover, whatever high-value dialog there is between the smart guys inside your company and the smart guys on the outside who want answers usually has a revenue stream attached to it: It's called technical support, and companies are predictably averse to compromising revenue streams.

But... what if it turns out that the *social* aspect of social media actually *is* important for geeks and how they make buying decisions, and yours is the one company that misses that very important boat by being late to the party? Plus, what if your competitors are actually saving money by introducing ways for customers to support each other rather than relying on expensive but non-differentiating support from you?

See the problem?

There's a terrific need to pin down the combatants in the ring long enough to get a decent look at them. More importantly, given the "Practical Insights" promise in the title, we'll focus on where to start sorting out the possible from the pitfalls, one step at a time.

Before we launch into details here, let's get back to the brutal honesty program mentioned earlier: We don't have all the answers neatly sewn up for you. This isn't because we haven't been paying attention, but rather because all the questions aren't yet known. We do, however, promise to share our experience, what we know to be true (so far), and what we know for sure you shouldn't even *think* about doing in your own social media program designed for your geek customers. So there's that.

So, Who's a Geek, Really?

Before we begin discussions about the "what" of a corporate social media program in a geek world, it makes sense to talk first about who is involved.

At the outset, let's agree that every study of human behavior by default demands a certain degree of simplification in order to be helpful. The risk is that simplifying categories of people, known in marketing circles as demographics, can easily prompt the accusation of stereotyping. Since the goal of this book is to understand social media as it relates to a specific type of person—those who purchase (or license) and use highly complex technical products and services—we want to say at the outset that the attributes we ascribe to geeks are not meant to be judgmental or hurtful in any way, nor are they intended to box individuals into rigid or overly-simplified definitions of the human experience. Having said that, if you are currently wearing a fanny pack and white socks with black shoes, have more than two electronic devices strapped to your body, or feel the compulsion to question exactly what we mean by "strapped to your body," chances are high you'll resonate with at least some of what follows.

And you'll be in good company. As of the publication of this book, a Google search for the keyword *"geek"* returns over 29 million results. Refine the search to *"geek definition"* and you still get more than 1.8 million results. Inquiring minds apparently want to know exactly what constitutes a geek. Let's start with a little (disturbing) history.

The term *geek* originally referred to carnival workers who earned their living by performing bizarre acts such as biting the heads off of chickens and snakes and eating glass.[2] Over time, it has come to be generally applied to anyone who earns their living in technical industries that the mainstream perceives as odd and/or incomprehensible. Currently, the Urban Dictionary defines geeks as, among other attributes, "The people you picked on in high school and wind up working for as an adult."[3]

According to the Internet-based consensus known as "Wikipedia,"[4] a geek is an enthusiast who is interested in technology and who "chooses concentration rather than conformity; one who passionately pursues skill (especially technical skill) and imagination, not mainstream social acceptance." Geeks manifest "a devotion to something in a way that places him or her outside the mainstream...due to the intensity, depth, or subject of their interest." In most circles, the term "geek" has transcended the pejorative color commonly associated with nerds, dweebs and dorks. Indeed, within fields such as engineering, physics, and mathematics, it is nothing less than a badge of honor to be regarded as a geek.

Specific to social media, there are numerous characteristics and attributes of the geek demographic that differentiate geek-to-geek (G2G) from business-to-business (B2B) and business-to-consumer (B2C) communities. These distinctions are significant for anyone launching or managing a social media program that targets geeks, because a healthy slice of the conventional wisdom espoused by B2C and B2B marketers may be irrelevant or unhelpful in geek environments.

So who are these geeks anyway, and what makes us think we know them?

The company we work for was founded by übergeeks. This is because we make much of the software that the semiconductor industry uses to design and manufacture integrated circuits (computer chips) and electronic devices of all kinds. As you might imagine, this can be an extremely complex process involving ridiculously complicated and systemically interdependent technologies and methodologies. In the words of Synopsys' co-founder, Chairman and CEO Aart de Geus, electronic design automation (EDA) is "the heart of the heart of the heart" of technology. As such, we employ and revere geeks—the geekier the better. Think, "The Humpty Dumpties of All the Eggheads on the Planet." They create the products and services we market and sell to other geeks (our customers). So in the spirit of full disclosure, the observations that follow are based on our own interactions over twenty-five combined years of hanging out with these folks, a smattering of research into the burgeoning and fascinating field of "geek studies," and insights shared with us by fellow observers in the geek world.

Geeks are by nature and training-analytical, logical, and precise. This results in conversation styles that resemble a serious commitment to truthfulness. According to Google CEO Eric Schmidt, in an article by Russ Mitchell of *U.S. News and World Report*:

> "One of the main characteristics of geeks is that they're very truthful," says Schmidt (who, in fact, uses the term "geek" only occasionally). "They're taught to think logically. If you ask engineers a precise question, they will give you a precisely truthful answer. That also tends to mean that they'll only answer the question that you asked them. If you don't ask them exactly the right question, sometimes they'll evade you—not because they're lying, but because they're being so scrupulously truthful."

A natural derivative of this orientation is that geeks tend to value being right over being liked. As you can imagine, this has important implications which we'll discuss later for those who intend to connect with them via social media and the plethora of "Like" buttons in social platforms and applications. There's an openness and lack of guile in most geeks that in some cases borders on painful to observe by those more skilled at the social games played by many. As a result, geeks tend to be pretty WYSIWYG (What You See Is What You Get), direct, and on occasion, tact-challenged.

In fairness, there is currently much debate in geek studies over whether or not social skill is a valid measure of "geekness." One camp claims that geeks can demonstrate perfectly "normal" social skills, and that it is more accurate to describe socially-challenged techno-fiends as "dorks," while the other side insists that by virtue of their intense interest in the correctness of things, geeks by default are doomed to be at least a little socially awkward. Regardless of where you land on this discussion, it's important to note that even if generally speaking geeks do care less than others about their own social acceptance based on typical measures of popularity, they still have egos and a desire for status. It's just that for geeks, their approval knobs tend to slide up and down on a scale of technical competence in problem solving. They have a passion for reason, and for them, the most important question is, "How does it work?" This is a critical aspect to keep in mind when developing a robust social media offering for your geeks that will garner high levels of engagement.

I Can't Get Past "Geek"

I have spent my professional life working with and around some of the greatest engineers and engineering cultures in the world; first at Thomas Edison's General Electric Company, then Jack Kilby's Texas Instruments, and Anton and Gerard Philips', NV Philips. I spend considerable time and effort understanding these remarkable individuals.

I'll admit engineers are logical, analytical, quantitative, and fact-based. They epitomize the rational being through analysis and logical dissection of everything. They're critical and realistic, love numbers, and know how things work. So to the rest of us, they're different, even a bit scary. You do have to communicate with them differently than you would a mere mortal. But in working with engineers, I came to the realization that engineers and scientists make things; the rest of us are parasites that live off what they make!

Our world has advanced and grown due to scientific discovery and advances in technology. The wheel, printing press, light, electricity, internal combustion engine, transistor, medicines, materials, rocketry, integrated circuit, computers, software, the Internet to name a few. And who made these advances possible???? GEEKS!!! Geeks? No, engineers did. Without engineers, we'd still be hunting wild animals with spears and living in caves.

Engineers built this country on innovation and technology. So why are we still dependent on oil? What other things are broken? Environment. Economy. Infrastructure. Education.

Today, the United States is graduating less than 10 percent of the world's engineers. And there is a greater than 50 percent mortality rate for engineering majors in our colleges and universities. My grandchildren's friends tell me they don't like math and science. "It isn't fun," they say. No math and science, no engineers, no new technology, no world leadership. Our overworked, underpaid, and underappreciated school teachers cannot be expected to make math and science fun and exciting. But, what if we get the Baby Boomer engineers to spend their retirement bringing the old character, "Mr. Wizard," back into the classroom?

> Engineers may be geeky, but they should never be referred to as "geeks." There is nothing in our lives that has not been made possible by engineers and scientists. The book you are holding explains how to best communicate with these very special people. Use that knowledge to help them do their jobs more efficiently. And let's bring math, science, engineering, and innovation back, and begin solving world problems before it's too late.
>
> *H. Buford Barr*
> *High-Tech electronics and B2B practitioner,*
> *now Lecturer in Marketing, Santa Clara University*

One characteristic of geeks that's frequently overlooked is that most place a high value on creativity, and specifically, their own creativity in problem-solving. If you want to ask the question, "What motivates a geek?" (and you definitely should be asking that question if you're trying to harness social media to create meaningful conversations with them!), then consider asking the question, "What motivates geeks to be creative?" In general, the answer never rests in externally motivating incentives, but rather in a passion for the work itself and the ability to push personal limits of exploration and creation.

Geeks also love a good thinking model. In geeks' eyes, everything is part of a system of other things, and in order to fully understand anything (and we know how important that is), they need to understand *what* and *how* it fits into the bigger picture. Efforts to educate or influence geek thinking outside a schema or process or thinking model will inevitably flounder. Challenging a geek to deconstruct a problem rationally is like putting peanut butter in front of a chipmunk—they almost can't help themselves. Find a way to weave that kind of hook into your geek social media program, and you'll have a winner for sure.

Another important characteristic, especially within the younger geek community, is that while money is important (and they get plenty of it, almost twice as much on average, in fact, as their counterparts in non-tech roles), believing that they're making a positive impact on the world is of equal, if not greater, importance. They believe in the value of their ideas, and they're competitive insofar as wanting to see their ideas "win."

While the immediate impact of this on their professional social media levels of engagement is not completely obvious, it's certainly an aspect of the demographic that could prove to be important down the road. Embedded in that statement is another interesting characteristic of the demographic: While you won't find many geeks chatting on Facebook about the complex and proprietary problems they're working on, that doesn't mean they don't use social media in their private lives, or that they won't share non "company confidential" solutions to problems in support forums. Where they do participate, they're proud of the techno-whiz reputations they develop online.

Social media provides virtual opportunities to like-minded individuals to build community, and geeks are no different than anyone else in that regard. Sometimes you want to go where everybody knows your name; but for geeks, the value of current social media opportunities for *professional* community building is less clear. A research project conducted by a team of students at Santa Clara University in mid-2010, for example, found that engineering geeks continue to overwhelmingly prefer email over all other communication channels. The research, which focused on 165 DesignCon 2010 conference attendees and 74 Synopsys Users Group (SNUG) participants, indicates that a substantial majority of these electrical engineers do not follow blogs, most reserve Facebook for personal (not professional) use, and most have scant interest (if any) in social media platforms such as Twitter.

Given such research-based insights, a G2G social media program that places all of its emphasis on blasting marketing messages through blogs or Facebook advertising or a strong Twitter presence is likely to miss the mark today, not to mention that geeks hate marketing spew. A different approach to engaging geeks via social media is needed, and frankly, it's one that's still not entirely clear in focus. But, we are getting close to knowing which questions to ask, and perhaps it's our own inner geek that leads us to this thinking, but knowing which questions to ask is a huge part of solving any problem.

So this brings us to the second "who" involved in this picture: you. Since the purpose of this book is to provide a solid foundation and some great questions to answer around G2G social media, who is it that might be looking for help with that?

Incoming Marketers

Nobody needs to give recent college graduates a tutorial on how to use Facebook or retweet a Twitter message. Generation Y has come of age in a technology-pervasive, interconnected world. For them, social media is already second nature and part of the "background of obviousness" with regard to how people communicate. What may not be immediately obvious when entering the professional workforce for the first time, however, is how much has changed in recent years for those who have been around awhile. Senior managers at geek companies have built their success in paradigms that have not included social media—originally because it didn't exist and lately because it may not be completely clear why it matters to the specific business they're managing. If you're in the Gen Y category, you can skim past the details about stuff you already know about social media and focus more on the context and historical perspective in the pages that follow.

Experienced Communicators

You've been in the workforce since the time when neither "friend" nor "unfollow" were considered verbs. You've built a successful career in marcom, PR, or other communications-related role, and one day your boss asks you to take the lead in running the social media program for your company or add a social media dimension to the marketing program you currently manage. In either case, this book is definitely for you. Although you're already Internet-savvy and social media-aware, what will you do to quickly get a handle on all the moving parts in a full-blown G2G social media program? What are the high-level considerations that compose the architecture of a coherent G2G initiative? Where is the terrain likely to present challenges? When venturing into uncharted territory for the first time as the one who's supposed to know, a bit of experienced guidance can smooth out some bumps from the learning curve ahead.

Traditional Marketers

Social media isn't your thing, and maybe it never will be. But maybe you still have some professional curiosity about what all the social media hoopla is all about. Surely there must be something more to it than reading blogs or experimenting with Twitter. By providing a detailed overview of what it takes to conceive and manage an end-to-end social media program that helps to effectively engage geeks, this book will help provide a contextual framework to help you understand what your non-traditional social media colleagues down the hall are up to—and why it potentially matters.

Corporate Managers

Your job is to run the business of whatever business you're in. You're aware of social media and may have even heard an anecdotal success story or two, but you're inclined to trust your marketing staff to sort through whatever implications social media may have for your business. If this is you—and you're holding this book—odds are that someone on your staff wants you to have a working familiarity with the framework and issues involved as social media takes root with the geek customers and markets your company serves.

As a matter of full disclosure, we do not claim status as a pure-play geek ourselves. We do, however, manifest many geeky characteristics we're rather proud of (like choosing concentration over conformity and passionately pursuing skill and imagination over mainstream social acceptance). Luckily for us, we possess just enough geekyness in mind and spirit to see the forest and the trees, as well as the human beings who are the substance of the pages that follow.

Oh, To Be A Geek

"My three (now grown) kids were sitting around the dinner table with me and my wife. They were parked right in the middle of their teen years, when poking fun at Mom and Dad had special appeal. Part of that process, of course, was correcting your parents' misuse of vernacular and other anthropological errors.

So, in my feeble attempt to be self-effacing, I referred to myself as a "nerd." This precipitated rolling eyes of disbelief and hysterical laughter that, frankly, caught me off guard. I thought to myself, "How else should I describe myself to appear regular and culturally aware of my kids' perception of me?" The surprised look was picked up be my eldest and she offered, "Dad, you're not a nerd. Mom is a nerd. You're a dork."

"A dork?" I said. "Yes, Mom's a nerd because of how much she loves school (she's an MD). You're a dork because you think you're cool, but you're not." I queried, "Can't I at least be a geek?" To which she replied, "No. A geek is a person that loves gadgets and tech stuff more than hanging' with people. They're way better than dorks; but, you're too into people and not that into gadgets. So, you're stuck with being a dork 'cause you're not cool."

If only I could be a geek.

Jack Harding
Chairman, President and CEO
eSilicon

Chapter 1

Stop

First Things First

As we discussed in the introduction, geek demographics are not the same as general business or broad-based consumer demographics, and this distinction has all kinds of implications for anyone tasked with starting and/or managing a geek-to-geek social media program. The engineering geeks who literally invented the Internet are typically not early adopters of the interactive/interpersonal potential the Internet makes possible. But, just because their adoption rate isn't high (yet) for most social media technologies, that doesn't mean that no geeks are using them.

Beginning at square one on the yellow brick road to G2G social media success, it's helpful to know as much as you can about the people who actually compose the community you wish to join. As an important aside, notice we didn't say "the target market you want to sell stuff to" or even "the audience you plan to talk to." Social media is all about engaging and conversing in multi-directional online conversations. For anyone in the marketing profession, we're hoping that's not a news flash.

From the beginning, some have looked at social media as a slick new channel to "get their message out," perhaps in the same way pupa-phase spammers took the measure of email when that channel was brand new. But that's not the way to go. If social media is a conversation (which it is), then spam is an interruption—so why do that? Better to join the party as a welcome participant than show up as a gate crasher. Even better, host a great party yourself and invite in all the geeks you can find, get the beer flowing, and then sit back and listen. We all have a lot to learn about these folks.

Whom do they trust? How do they communicate? What types of information do they value? Where do they congregate? What lights their fire, or turns them off? The more you know about who "they" are and how they prefer to interact, the potentially smoother your entree into an environment that you didn't define and certainly don't control.

Who Goes There?

Like shapes in the fog, a clear and definitive snapshot of how geeks engage with social media is challenging to discern. One reason is that anecdotal perspectives tend to skew the view in one direction or another (and are typically more accurate in describing corner cases than the core of the overall bell curve).

Listen to a social media enthusiast, for example, and one gets the impression that late adopters are missing a very important ticket to making their relationships deeper, networks stronger, and lives profoundly better (who knows, maybe they're right). Of course, that's the fundamental nature of enthusiasm: great excitement for a subject or cause. As such, looking at the world through the rose-colored glasses of enthusiasm is not the same as applying an objective business lens to form an unbiased snapshot.

Opposite the enthusiast end of the spectrum live traditionalists who generally aren't all that open to change or new ways of doing things. Quick to dismiss social media with an "I don't care what size latte you're ordering right now" wave of the hand, traditionalists look at the world through spectacles (even blinders) of their own.

So, who's right? The answer is, both...and neither. Both perspectives are able to accurately describe the points on the continuum they most understand and/or relate to, but neither speaks for the whole.

So here you are at step one—simply trying to understand the traits and communication preferences of the geek community you want to engage—and already it's complicated. Isn't there some objective, third-party research out there that can sort all this out?

Paint Me a Picture

Beyond opinions and anecdotes, the other reason it's challenging to form a clear picture of how geeks engage with social media is that primary research targeting various slices of the B2B and G2G markets often yields remarkably different results and conclusions, often leading to more questions than clarity.

Consider, for example, a report authored by Laura Ramos titled "Rethinking the B2B Tech Marketing Mix in the Digital Age"[5] (Forrester Research, March 2010). Based on a research sample of 249 B2B marketers at companies with fifty or more employees, she wrote:

> "Social media became the hot new marketing tool. Penetrating even the most conservative marketing organizations, social networking, microblogging, and blog publishing shifted the B2B marketing mix significantly toward digital channels in 2009. For the first time, this survey looked at the role that applications like Facebook, LinkedIn, and Twitter play in the mix, and we found B2B marketers flocking to set up shop in these communities to converse with potential buyers. Two-thirds of B2B marketers (68%) have established group pages on social networking sites, exceeding inside sales use by 3%. Barely a blip on our 2008 radar screen, more than half of respondents (55%) said they now use Twitter for marketing purposes. Almost half (49%) employ corporate blogging, a number much higher than the 32% who embraced this digital medium in 2008."

Sounds like social media went mainstream for tech marketers in 2009. But wait, the tech marketing subset of B2B is not a homogeneous demographic: A PC manufacturer that sells laptops to a corporate procurement department is certainly a B2B tech marketer, but quite different from a G2G tech marketer that sells low-power optimization software solutions to chip design engineers. So while research focused on B2B tech marketing may be more relevant to the geek world than generic B2C research, G2G companies are advised to consider both as potentially informative, but neither as conclusive.

Dive Deeper

Step by step, the shapes in the fog become progressively more discernible. Sifting further into the survey data gathered by the student researchers at Santa Clara University referenced in the introduction, the following insights emerge from those surveyed:

- Of those who responded, only 10 percent of DesignCon attendees and *zero* SNUG participants use Twitter

- Although 57 percent have Facebook accounts, most reserve Facebook for personal (not professional) use

- LinkedIn has achieved the highest adoption rate among engineers: 63 percent

- 59 percent of DesignCon and 53 percent of the surveyed SNUG attendees stated that the proprietary nature of their jobs inhibits their participation in online forums

In addition to surveying engineering geeks in the current workforce, the researchers also interviewed a group of twenty-eight electrical engineering majors at the School of Engineering at Santa Clara University. The researchers note, "While the current generation of engineers had to adopt the use of online sites and resources mid-career, the next generation of engineers has already adopted the Internet and everything it has to offer." Even so, although 100 percent of the EE majors surveyed have Facebook accounts, none interact with blogs, none have Twitter accounts and only 11 percent use LinkedIn.

Synopsys conducted a research study in March 2010 among current users of EDA software. Based on 1,867 completed surveys, the research underscores a consideration noted in the last bullet point above (a factor that's virtually non-existent in the B2C world and of peripheral concern in B2B communities): Corporate policies sometimes restrict participation in online technical communities—even those directly germane to an employee's professional role.

Corroborating another part of the Santa Clara University findings, *EE Times* found that Twitter usage among engineering geeks is decisively low. The geek-focused publisher conducted a survey in May 2010 that asked "What's your gut reaction to Twitter?"

In her blog post that analyzes the results, Karen Field writes:[6]

> The results from 285 survey respondents revealed that 85 percent don't use Twitter. More than half indicated that the statement "I don't really care what you had for breakfast," best sums up their feelings about it; others characterized it as "a ridiculous waste of time and electrons" or expressed the strong desire for it to simply "go away."

Field quotes Jeffrey Tuttle, a hardware design engineer, as saying, "'The amount of information in a tweet is not worth the time spent looking at it... To be productive when doing design, you need long periods of uninterrupted thought. Twitter by its nature is intrusive and interruptive. Consequently it seems to be for those people who don't have enough to do.'"

Jeffrey's stated opinion is an interesting confirmation of the assessment that geeks care more about the value of information and productivity at work than they do about the experience of connecting with other people. And he's not alone in holding this opinion.

A significant number of engineers evidently see little value to their professional standing to checking in, hanging out, or building online ties with potential peer groups. Ironically, even among geeks who *are* actively engaged in social media, some hold "generic" social media in disregard if not downright disdain.

For example, in his blog post of August 29, 2010, technology blogger and self-proclaimed geek Daniel Nenni wrote:[7]

> "Why will everybody in the entire world have a smartphone and/or tablet PC in the not too distant future? One word, NARCISSISM! What else drives the masses to Facebook, YouTube, Twitter, WordPress, FailBlog, Blah, Blah, Blahblahblah... All key enablers of the mobile Internet explosion."

Currently then, it appears that the best that *certain* social media technologies can hope to do in the G2G space is to help create a positive predisposition so that when other things happen downstream, there's a favorable mindset of receptivity. That mindset is developed not only from social media, but from every other touch-point in the ecosystem. Did they hear your CEO speak recently, and how did that go? Do they like, trust, and respect their sales rep? Did they feel paid attention to when they had a problem, and was the problem resolved to their satisfaction? As we'll see in future chapters, it's very difficult to map direct causes and effects in the social media space, particularly in the G2G domain.

We believe all of this to be true, but does that mean we simply shouldn't bother with a social media program at all? No! We definitely should bother, and give it our very best shot while we're at it, and here's why:

First, one of the key values of Twitter is that it gives us the ability to "listen to the buzz." For example, several of our product marketing teams listen to the downstream buzz about what's working/not in their domains (and even what's coming with the standards under development). There's a *lot* of Twitter traffic in these areas, and listening in provides excellent and necessary reconnaissance to a marketer and product manager (and the R&D team as well).

Second, while applications such as Facebook and Twitter seem to hold little appeal (although certainly more than zero) to the majority of the geek world as it relates to their professional care-abouts, other media such as blogs, technical forums, and even YouTube hold significant promise in the G2G world. Think about those geek attributes we discussed earlier: Anything that has the potential to assist geeks in being more creative in their technical problem-solving, or build a more robust perspective of the big picture in which they're trying to solve those problems, or even find a more interesting place or team or set of problems to work with can be of immense value.

And maybe that's why even Facebook and Twitter shouldn't be underestimated regardless of evidence to the contrary. One of the interesting aspects of the *EE Times* survey described above is the favorable and outspoken passion expressed by the 15 percent of engineers who participated in the survey who do use Twitter. In response to the previously mention blog post by *EE Times*' Karen Field titled "Why Engineers Hate Twitter," Synopsys' Karen Bartleson commented, "I'm an engineer and I absolutely love Twitter. I use it every day. It's a powerful communication channel that helps me constantly with my work and outside activities. I know quite a few other engineers who love it, too. We're capitalizing on technology that we engineers invented, after all."

While the bulk of other engineers may not (yet) agree with Bartleson on the value of Twitter, she has apparently found (and one might argue, built) a community of like-minded geek communicants who find their perception of their work world informed, enhanced, and enriched by their engagement online.

Zoom Back Out

With each wave of data, the shapes become clearer, even if they're but a snapshot of a moving target. As helpful as research data may be, however, there's only so much enlightenment one is likely to find down in the weeds. At some point, the most helpful view only snaps into focus from the 10,000-foot level, where the entire forest becomes visible.

More than any other specific research finding about geek communication preferences, the Twitter vignette just described may be the most significant marker of all for what geek companies should understand about geek communities and social media: Some love it, some hate it... and most are focused on other interests.

But even if only a small fraction of the community is latching onto one aspect of social media or another, the smallest handful is still worth paying attention to. Let's say, for example, the furthest reaches of your universe consists of just 100,000 current and potential customers. If only 10 percent of the total available market is tapped into Twitter, that's still 10,000 people—enough to fill more than twenty Boeing 747s.

While that's not everybody, it's still an impressive number. Plus, any cohesive subset of a larger group that's willing to buck the status quo of the majority is likely to hold sway beyond their numbers. What if these 10 percent are the influencers? Early adopters? Evangelists? The people who bridge communities? This is definitely a good group to connect with.

First-Hand Experience

Beyond well-intended anecdotes and whatever research you might be able to find, the most valuable information source of all is usually first-hand experience. At Synopsys, we launched a social media program in 2007. Sometimes through trial and error, occasionally through inspiration, but mostly through the methods described in this book, the program has grown into a nexus for interaction with the übergeeks EDA community.

With experience comes knowledge, and web metrics help to inform some of what we know. Synopsys blogs, for example, are viewed by close to 5,000 unique visitors a month. Undaunted by research to the contrary, we know for sure that a significant number of engineering geeks do read blogs and, specifically, they're reading Synopsys blogs. Even in the absence of web analytics metrics, simply look around. Go to a technical conference or geek trade show, and you'll see Internet-connected/social media-enabled mobile devices everywhere. Go on-line to LinkedIn, Twitter or Facebook, and you'll see impressive numbers of geeks self-associating with geek groups and geek brands at every turn.

Look backwards: Usenet (an Internet-based discussion system) has been around since 1980—more than a decade before the World Wide Web was hatched—and geeks have been a core constituency of that computer-based communications system from the get-go. Look ahead: Companies of every size are investing increasingly more and diverting a larger percentage of their shrinking marketing/PR spend on social and other electronic media on the bet that social media is here to stay—whether that reflects a "build it and they will come" mentality or a forward-looking business acumen, critical mass and time are on their side either way.

As sure as the Internet genie will never be put back into the bottle, social media is not going away. It's got a solid foothold—yes, even among geeks—that's irreversible. With that, it's time to advance to Job #2: Observe the lay of the land before you pitch your tent.

Are you an engineer-geek?

Do you remember the line from the movie "Forest Gump" where Forest's mom assured him that if God wanted all people to be special he would have created them all needing braces on their feet to walk straight? Or Captain Kirk of "Star Trek" fame passing the "Kobiashi Maroon" test by changing the rules (cheating)?

If you possess the combination of the illogical reasoning of the first with the brilliance of the second—and add a heavy dose of self-confidence and a belief of possessing a monopoly on flawless thinking...Then there is a good chance you are an engineer-geek!

If you simultaneously believe that disorder could result from perfect order (you call it random variability)—and that perfect order could come out of disorder (you call it clever engineering)...you are a good candidate for being an engineer-geek.

Let me give you an example: In optical wafer processing the wavelength of the light used couldn't keep up with ruthless continuous feature shrinking engineers are bent on pursuing, so the resulting printed shrunk shapes started getting heavily distorted. How did engineer-geeks solve the problem and "cheat" light? They distorted the original drawn shapes in a calculated way so that when light distorts the distorted shape you end up with a good shape. It reminds me of the kid's joke: How do you know when sour cream goes bad? It tastes sweet!

If you judge your kids' school tournaments as if you are grading a PhD thesis…you are a good engineer-geek candidate.

Finally, to qualify as an engineer-geek candidate you should see no need for marketing or sales, and think of both functions as totally unnecessary.

Jamil Kawa
Engineering Group Director, Implementation Group
Synopsys

STONE AGE SOCIAL MEDIA PLATFORM EVALUATION

Chapter 2
Look

Chapter 1 focused on getting to know your community by noticing what makes them distinctive and observing their collective predispositions with regard to social media. This chapter advances the process of observation still further by considering the style, customs, and nuances of the social fabric you aim to join. The idea here is to stroll before you troll.

Note at the outset, we didn't say "...**brand** of the social fabric you aim to join." It's an important distinction to nail down at the outset of a discussion about what you want to observe as you do your strolling. As the saying goes, if all you have is a hammer, everything looks like a nail. And to traditional marketers accustomed to thinking of everything they do as a branding opportunity, social media platforms look deliciously like a bazillion opportunities for brand impressions.

People have personalities. Companies have brands. Social media communities have cultures.

While the opportunity to reinforce, enhance, and inform your corporate brand certainly exists through social media (as we'll see in subsequent chapters), it's generally a better idea to initially explore the opportunity space from the perspective of entering a neighborhood and feeling out the culture, rather than sashaying into a party of strangers looking for your opportunity to make a big splash. It's a subtle yet fundamentally important shift in perspective.

Look Before You Leap

Imagine sitting in the passenger seat of an airplane and deciding that you'd like to become a pilot. How likely would you be to unbuckle your seat belt, walk to the cockpit door, knock and say "Move over and let me fly this contraption?"

OK, so plunging head first into geek-to-geek social media from a cold start won't result in an unexpected nose dive from 30,000 feet, but there are several reasons why it's a good idea to begin your journey into social media for geeks by being an observer first and a participant second.

As an observer, you can get to know the online customs and etiquette practiced by those who have been at it for a while so that, when you're ready to engage, you're less likely to appear like a bull in a china shop. Surf the web and notice which blogs you like (and the ones you don't) and why. Are you impressed by Twitter users who present a steady diet of press releases, or do you prefer tweets that reflect a bit of personality? How about online ads: welcome or unwelcome? Valuable or obtrusive?

As you make observations, try to do so through a geek lens. If you are a bona fide geek, piece of cake. If you're a non-geek working at a geek company, apply what you know about your geek colleagues, managers, and customers to guide your assessments about what's appropriate for your specific program and situation.

By taking the time to get to know and understand the lay of the land before undertaking a social media program of your own, you'll be that much more ready when it comes time to take the leap live and in person for all the world to see.

Geeks. You say it like it's a bad thing...

I'm a life-long geek who was asked to take on the role as head-marketer for a $1.4 Billion company four years ago. The only reason this makes any sense at all is that all of our customers are geeks too. All of them. Some are basket cases.

We make IC design software. Our customers are some of the smartest and nicest people in the world. They're not all great at a cocktail party, but neither are we.

So how do we market to these folks? Simple: geek-to-geek. First you need a head geek. This had better be someone who doesn't set off any "anti-geek" alarms in your customer base. (Have they ever played a sport? Bad sign. Golf and football are absolute disqualifiers. Also anything else.) We're lucky that our CEO, who started the company (big plus in the geek community), is a particular breed of over-achieving, hyper-precise...gentleman (fearing for my job, I won't use the word geek here!). Aart de Geus (our CEO—and doesn't the name get us halfway there?) is a super-nice, thoughtful übergeek (OK, I said it). Aart is a master public-speaker who wows the crowds with the depth and complexity of his talks, leaving our audiences in a sort of collective after-glow of what is possible in the highest levels of geek achievement.

So, you need a guy like this. He's your figurehead. Don't send the ex-football guy out there. Or anyone from Sales. They make the geeks feel bad because they're not him.

Next you need to avoid anything that seems like "marketing." To geeks, marketing is just telling a set of obvious lies ("wear this stinky smell, and women will love you—even though you're you"). Geeks are too smart for that. They're cynical and suspicious. They won't believe anything your corporation says. If you must say something, you could try a combination of Joe Friday ("Just the facts, ma'am"), Spock ("The logic is elemental"), and John Belushi ("Guess what I am now").

> Better is to talk to them geek-to-geek. Have your geeks talk to them about what works. Once their bona-fides are established, your geeks are credible. They can't be lying because they're equally cynical. A true geek could never tell a lie to another geek with a straight face.
>
> Geek-to-geek marketing is the way of the future. Geeks are just ahead of the curve. The era of mass-market advertising lasted about 50 years, but it's over now, and it wasn't killed by DVRs and the web. It was killed because no one believes a word they hear in an advertisement. Geeks knew that a long time ago, and now everyone else is getting it too.
>
> *John Chilton*
> *Senior VP Marketing & Corporate Development*
> *Synopsys*

Best Practices

While in observer mode, keep an eye out for opportunities to document "best practices" for the social media program you're developing. Best practices help to achieve and maintain alignment within teams by creating a common understanding of the constituent parts of the overall program, and they're invaluable in helping to orient new people who may join the team at a later time.

Best practices can be captured and documented in formats ranging from formal policies (see Social Media Policy in Chapter 3) to informal guidelines for internal use within your own team. "How to" guides can be particularly useful as a way of articulating specific processes or expectations for a social media program. It's easy to imagine how a guide that answers questions like "What's the ideal frequency to publish new blog posts?" or "What's the escalation path to resolve a negative comment?" can be useful, especially in those rare but heart-stopping moments when some customer guano hits the fan.

> **Geek Eureka!**
>
> Geek managers are fond of tables and bullet-point lists (check boxes are a particular favorite among some), so consider the preferences of the people who will use the document when developing a format.

Learn from Other People's Mistakes

The best way to learn from a mistake is to let somebody else make an error that you learn something from. If you're building a social media program from the ground up, there will be plenty of opportunities to learn from your own mistakes. But why not take note of some of the more obvious stuff there is to learn while you're still in observer mode?

What kind of mistakes can one learn from? Some are universally obvious: If the primary goal of your social media interactions is to promote your corporate brand, then posting inflammatory content anywhere is almost certainly a bad idea. Any violation of company policies is always a mistake (e.g., discussing confidential or proprietary information in a public forum, which can actually get you sent to jail). Remember that the rules for conduct in the "real world" apply with equal weight in the online world, and maybe even more so, as transgressions in the realm of social media can be "shared" with glee anywhere in the world in seconds. Note to social media managers: "Going viral" isn't always a good thing.

Of course, universal mistakes don't always announce themselves through bullhorns. Take, for example, a blog that languishes on a corporate site month after month, apparently abandoned. It's hard to argue how that's not a mistake in the form of a missed opportunity (at best), or a disregard for the reader (at worst), who comes away feeling like a loser who's interested today in a topic that clearly no one, not even the author, cares about any longer.

Other mistakes are more in the eye of the beholder, so we'll call them "preferences of note." The question of how much (or how little) individual personality to put into a corporate blog is largely a matter of subjective opinion, although there have been some interesting developments lately of "celebrity" corporate bloggers who, upon leaving a company, actually take with them a sizable proportion of a company's blog readership. This has led to revised corporate opinions on the wisdom of allowing a strong personality or voice to be created in a corporate blog.

Other questions will surface. Is it better to hold user comments for moderation before publishing, or to allow such comments to be posted real time and deal with potential nastiness as it comes up? The answer is one of subjective preference, resource bandwidth, management style, or all of the above. The point here is that prior to landing on an approach to your own social media program, form conscious assessments about what you notice as an observer first. How do *you* feel about having a comment held back until it has been approved, and more importantly, how do you think your geek community would feel? By navigating through a wide variety of social media platforms as a conscious observer of yourself while also wearing a geek community member hat, you'll begin to develop a good feel for what should and shouldn't be part of the community culture you eventually hope to host.

One additional category of mistakes has to do with not knowing what you don't know. This is a tough category by definition, but one's odds can be improved by searching for answers even when the questions themselves are unclear. It would be a mistake, for example, to launch a social media program with no consideration about how to measure success. Ah, but that's why you're reading this book, and we hope the chapters ahead will help.

Apply a Geek Filter

Go to any social media conference or thumb through just about any social media-related book, and you're bound to find examples and success stories from the B2C and B2B worlds that may have little or no relevance to geeks. So while you're gathering information and making observations about what's gone before, it will be useful to apply a geek filter on the range of possibilities you find.

If it's true that one size does not fit all (it's actually true), then lessons learned the Motrin Moms, Best Buy or "Will it blend?" YouTube videos will be only marginally instructive as you develop a geek-to-geek social media plan. Focus more on what seems to be working in online venues closer to the professional interests of your target audience—and save the attempt to create the next viral video until once the core of your program is soundly established.

Shades of Originality

As you're making "I like this and I don't like that" decisions, what do you do with the concepts and ideas you really like? You can't just steal other people's work. Even if you could, you probably wouldn't want to become a me-too follower who lacks original ideas of your own.

That's not to say it's somehow illegal or in bad taste to be influenced by the work of others. With regard to the architecture of a web site, there's not much new under the sun that can, or should, be called totally original. Most navigation systems, for example, have some version of "Home," "Search" and "Contact Us," and blog platforms like WordPress and Blogger feature widgets and design templates that all but ensure some level of consistency and commonality (unoriginality?) from site to site. That's OK, even desirable. If every navigation system were totally different, for example, the web would be a less efficient space as users stumbled through one expression of originality after another. And your geek community already understands all about the value of standards and won't thank you for making them think about elements they consider should be intuitively obvious.

Rather, think about the time spent as investing in building a thinking model for your social media program, based on the principles and patterns that bubble up from the specifics. Of the things you stumble on that you really like, is there a common thread, higher-level principle, or architecture of approach that begins to emerge? In other words, how are you going to think about your social media program?

For example, it's sometimes helpful in building a thinking model of anything to boil it down to the "Journalist Six." In this case, the six questions journalists always use to piece together a story might look like this:

- **Who** will you attempt to reach and bring into your conversation? Who are the internal stakeholders? Who's already out there chatting about your products, industry issues, and visions for the future?

- **What** are they talking about? What topics hold the most interest for them? What holds the least? And what level of engagement seems most prevalent?

- **Where** are you finding them?

- **Why** are they there? Are they also in other spaces? If not, why not?

- **When** is the highest level of engagement visible?

- **How** are the most successful hosts out there working their magic?

That last question can be admittedly maddening to try to answer, but it's worth taking the time to observe and model what's happening, and why.

Through the process of observation, somewhere in the middle ground between things that you'll do the same, and things that you'll do totally differently will lie the unique voice that you'll bring to your own social media program. As you move forward, don't be afraid to be influenced by others whom you respect or who inspire you. It's OK to adopt an approach or style or world view you will find by surfing the web and then adapt it to your own purposes. Be creative with the adaptation—and be flattered when others do the same.

Miscommunication between Engineers and Marketing

Many times in industry, there is a total disconnect between engineers and the marketing team. What's at the core of this miscommunication?

Engineers enjoy and are motivated by finding new, unique, and creative ways of solving difficult technical problems. To an engineer who may have spent many hours trying to find a solution for a problem, there's a sense of pride in his or her accomplishments, like a piece of well-crafted art.

Often when the time comes to bring a product to market, the marketing team is brought up to speed on what the product does and how it works. The engineering team, of course, tries to highlight the new, unique, and creative ideas that are in the new product.

At this point the marketing team puts together its own view of what's important to make the product marketable. The results often don't sit well with the engineers: "How could those marketing folks be so out to lunch—I told them about the new, unique, and creative things that I put into this product and they didn't mention a one of them!"

The fundamental point is that each group dances to the beat of different drummer. Attributes that are especially rewarding to engineers may not have the same value to a marketing person. For a company to be successful, both groups' perspectives are needed. So remember that your way of looking at something is not necessarily the best way for the other group and that both views are needed for success. Hang in there!

Tom Williams
Inventor, Scientist, and IEEE Fellow

Chapter 3 Synchronize

Alignment

In order to set at least a quasi-realistic trajectory for your social media planning process, it's a huge help to seek initial alignment among the various stakeholders within your organization. Brace yourself: There are two predictable realities you can count on in this process:

1. There will be more people who consider themselves "stakeholders" than you currently think there are.
2. They will all have stronger opinions on the subject than you wish they did.

Maybe you're currently thinking a quick chat with PR, HR, the marcom folks and Sales should make up a decent starter set, but have you considered the brouhaha that will ensue if you neglect to loop in the perspectives of IT, Legal, Employee Communications, the web team, and Customer Support?

The reality is that total alignment can be a lofty goal within many organizations and, in many cases, unachievable.

There are many reasons why this may be the case, including (but not limited to):

- Legitimate concerns about likely discontinuities and potential business impacts
- Differences of opinion, perspective, or worldview
- No mandate for change within the organization(s)
- Lack of understanding or agreement regarding potential benefits
- Lack of motivation
- Fear of the unknown
- Fear of change
- Fear of loss of control
- Unfavorable anecdotal impressions
- Lack of trust or respect for the people leading the program
- Lack of regard for where the function sits within the organizational hierarchy
- Office politics
- Personal bias and/or a generalized mood of corporate crankiness
- Lack of time to gather all the opinions and/or gain agreement

Some of these barriers to alignment can be addressed through constructive engagement, education, or simply getting the right people in the same room to talk things through.

But be aware that most geek organizations have business-related care-abouts that the Zappos and 1-800-Flowers of the world don't. Proprietary intellectual property, for example, abounds inside companies that provide emerging technologies and throughout the companies that serve them. How does one safeguard confidential knowledge in a medium that's open and social by definition? (See the section on Social Media Policy below for some constructive recommendations.)

In addition, the business models of many geek companies consider "support" as a profit center (or at a minimum break-even), and have most likely operated successfully on that basis for years. Consider, for example, a company that sells specialized software by licensing seats for a defined period. If the terms of the license include access to a Help Center that can be contacted to assist in using or applying the software to a specific problem, the cost of providing such service (over and above the value of the software) will be built into the financial structure of the license agreement. The cost of staffing and operating a Help Center full of product experts is substantial, so such companies can't give away custom support for free. Yet "free" is a common expectation in the world of social media where peers help each other in user forums and other online venues that support threaded comments. And even if revenue is not at risk, what happens if well-meaning but under-educated users spread inaccurate information and seriously muck things up with *your* product? If you work at a geek company that fits this description, expect some creative tension between how things have always been done in the past and new ideas for how the underlying care-abouts might evolve in the future.

The good news is that even where total alignment isn't possible for a comprehensive social media plan (much less for the concept of social media itself), there are likely to be many areas where meaningful steps receive sufficient support to be acted upon. The important thing is to make progress towards alignment wherever possible while looking for pragmatic opportunities to make incremental progress where alignment is elusive or completely out of reach.

Nerds: Smart Kids Who Are Into Math

In Brooklyn, when I was growing up, we never had the term "geek." Instead, we called the smart kids who were into math and science "nerds."

I was a nerd.

> While other kids were in Drivers Ed class, I was in number theory class.
>
> In a high school known for its city championship sports teams, I was co-captain of the high school Math Team.
>
> While most of my peers picked their college from Playboy's Top Ten Party Schools, I chose my college by compiling a weighted average of evaluation criteria multiplied by average ratings taken from *US News*, *Time*, and *Forbes*.
>
> My friends told stories of wild parties at SUNY Binghamton. I told stories of wild "hacks" (like putting cows on top of domes and rolling Harvard kids across a bridge).
>
> The most popular movie in most other colleges was "Animal House." The most popular movie at MIT was anything by Monty Python.
>
> After all these years, I finally figured out that we nerds and geeks have a different "technical orientation." We know we're supposed to be like the rest of the world, but we're just "wired" differently than the rest of the world. But we're wired very similarly to each other. So when we geeks get together, we have plenty to talk about. Even using social media...you just have to speak our language.
>
> **Harry "the ASIC Guy" Gries**
> **Blogger, ASIC Methodology and EDA Technology Consultant**

Shared Expectations

It pays to get as many stakeholders as possible on the same page with regard to basic social media expectations. Taking the time to discuss and explore fundamental questions and develop a mutual understanding of the answers helps to improve business results, solidifies the shared sense of a common mission, and minimizes confusion and misunderstandings along the way.

To that end, here is a checklist of questions to address before diving head first into a social media program on behalf of your company:

"What" Questions:

- What problem are we trying to solve?
- What do we hope to gain? (What does success look like?)
- What do our customers want and/or expect?
- What unique value can we provide?
- What will it cost? What resources are needed?
- What are the potential risks and benefits?
- What's the cost of doing nothing?
- What roadblocks are we likely to encounter?

"Why" Questions:

- Why do we think social media is a good idea?
- Why do this?
- Why not?
- Why now?

"How" Questions:

- How will we distinguish ourselves in the social media space?
- How will we implement the social media plan?
- How will social media help us sell more stuff?
- How will we measure success?
- How will we deal with ugly situations?
- How will we avoid legal issues?

- How will we know if the program is working (or not working)?
- How much time and money will it take to build and maintain a successful program?
- How does social media fit with other parts of the company's marketing mix?

"Who" Questions:

- Who is responsible for the overall success of the program?
- Who does it makes sense to ask to deliver specific components of the program? (e.g., blogs, forum moderation, Web support)
- Who will the program engage? (e.g., customers, employees, shareholders)
- Who are the essential stakeholders within your organization?
- Who already does social media really well? (e.g., competitors, adjacencies)
- Who can help? (e.g., social media vendors, consultants, service providers)

The answers to these questions will be as various as the composition of the organizations that address them. Regardless of the specific responses, the process itself ensures a validated focus on what actions to pursue and why. The ability to articulate shared expectations encourages a proactive versus reactive approach to solving problems.

This is especially important for anyone who assumes responsibility for a social media program and its deliverables. Vague trajectories seldom improve through time. When detractors ask "What's the return-on-investment (ROI) of social media?" it will be valuable, perhaps even job-saving, to be able to answer with a response that maps back to how the program is performing in the context of a clearly defined and agreed set of expectations.

Trust and Respect

Beyond high-level alignment and a common understanding of specific expectations, the twin values of trust and respect are essential to the ultimate success of any social media program. Internally as well as externally, these values form a foundation without which even the most creative plan or slickest website will inevitably fail to reach their full potential.

Trust is metaphorically described as a bank account that one builds a single deposit at a time, and it is very much the coin of the realm online as in the rest of life. Trust equals credibility equals respect. Enough said.

Social Media Policy

Got an Internet connection? Got employees? You need a social media policy.

Just as a social media plan is a strategy document that defines objectives for the department tasked with its implementation, a social media policy is a procedural document that defines online conduct expectations across the company. Both require deliberation, review, and approval per the standard practices of the organization that adopts them. And both are essential to ensure synchronization of the program.

What are the rules of engagement? Where are the guardrails and boundaries? What forms of conduct are encouraged and which are unacceptable? From blogging to posting comments or videos to contributing to a wiki to tweeting, the purpose of the social media policy is to document the answers to such questions to help current and future employees understand what's expected of them when engaging with others online.

Some companies may elect to express policies as a set of rules with specific consequences, while others may opt to articulate expectations in terms of guidelines. At Synopsys, the policy guidelines are as follows:

Professional Conduct

Social media technologies are simply a way to facilitate conversations through a computer screen rather than in person. It is important for employees to act no differently using these technologies than they would when representing the Company at a physical event such as a trade show, standards committee meeting, or at a customer's facility. In addition, all communication through social media technologies must also conform to all other Company policies.

Identify Yourself

Online communities allow anonymity through the use of aliases. Our intent is to participate in these communities openly, so there is no need to hide that fact. Therefore, when participating in these various social networks and on-line communities, mark all of your contributions with your name and when relevant, your role at the Company.

Respect Copyright

Although the web makes it easy to copy and paste content between various sources, employees must understand and respect the copyrights of others. Any time content is reused from another source, make sure to attribute such content to the rightful copyright holder. Better still, use hyperlinks to link to the original content source whenever possible.

Don't Tell Secrets

Never publish or otherwise disclose confidential or proprietary information belonging to the Company or other entities.

Seek Permission

Never quote or reference customers, employees, partners, or suppliers without their approval.

Respect the Community

Employees are expected to always treat others with respect and never use obscenity, ethnic slurs, or make personal attacks. Avoid topics that may be considered objectionable or inflammatory—such as politics and religion. If you must disagree, disagree respectfully.

Do Not Vandalize

Due to the "Read/Write" nature of the web, it is possible for people to cause mischief on websites such as a Wiki. Although it may be tempting to use the anonymity of the web to make false claims, any such employee actions are strictly prohibited.

Fix Mistakes

If you've made a mistake, be the first to correct it. If you must alter a post, indicate that you have done so by "lining out" text that's stricken from your post.

Be Interesting

Be knowledgeable in your field. Write interesting posts, be relevant, and stay on topic.

Check Your Work

Quality matters. Check your facts before you post. Run your post through a spell checker. Finally, before you push that submit button...check one more time!

Personal Responsibility

Employees are personally responsible for the content they post on the Internet. Please be aware that anything you publish on the Internet may be publicly available indefinitely.

Common Sense

Prior to publishing company-related content on the Internet, ask yourself the following three questions:

- *Is this an important topic to the Company?*
- *Is it in the Company's interest to get involved in this particular topic?*
- *Am I qualified and/or authorized to publicly address this topic?*

Never discuss pricing decisions, roadmaps, unannounced financial results, predictions of future performance, or similar matters that could get you, the Company, or both, into serious legal trouble. If you are unsure about posting any particular content, refrain from posting.

If these guidelines work for your company exactly as written, great! Use them in good health. If not, do not turn the page until you start on one of your own. At the time of this writing, a great resource for those in the policy writing stage is http://socialmediagovernance.com/policies.php

Regardless of where you get your ideas from, write your policy. As a final note, once you've gone to all the trouble to create your social media policy, share it!

According to a May 2010 study[8] of 100 companies by marketing firm Digital Brand Expressions, 78 percent of corporate respondents say their company is using social media, while only about half (41 percent) of those that do say they have a strategic plan in place to guide their efforts. Even more surprising:

> …even for the firms that do have a strategic plan in place, only 29 percent reported distributing policies and/or communications protocols to employees. This leaves the majority of organizations exposed to problems arising from employees saying the wrong things in the wrong ways to the wrong people at the wrong time.

Weird, eh? There's no mention in the study of the specific industries involved, but we're pretty sure they weren't geeks. We're much smarter than that, aren't we?

Geeks Have Always Used Social Media

We invented it.

We were the first to use Bulletin Boards.

We were the first to use CompuServe.

We were the first to use the web—...before graphical browsers. Remember Linx?

As pragmatic beings, geeks use tools to accomplish things. Period.

If Twitter doesn't work for us, we'll find another real-time application that does.

You see, to geeks, the actual "social medium" doesn't matter.

It's what we can do with it that does.

Ron Ploof
Author: Read This First: The Executive's Guide to New Media—From Blogs to Social Networks

Chapter 4 Plan

Why Plan?

The process of creating a social media plan should begin with a rough idea of what you want to accomplish (based on your insight-pulling conversations with your key stakeholders) and end with a strategic roadmap that has been shopped around with enough of those same people to form a consensus for action.

In between those two endpoints you'll discover where gaps exist in your initial thinking model, who agrees with what, and why some things that seem easy at first glance turn out to be hard (and vice versa).

By now you will have already discovered the seemingly easy—yet deceptively hard-twin questions "Why are we doing this?" and "What, specifically, are we hoping to accomplish?"

Are you diving into social media to become a thought leader in your slice of whatever industry you're in, or to save a bundle in user support costs, or because someone up your management chain thinks he or she can smell a terrific marketing opportunity? Or, is your company simply worried about appearing to be asleep at the wheel by not participating in the biggest online social phenomenon since the Internet began?

Land Grab

Early in our fledgling social media days at Synopsys, we experienced a few interesting adrenaline-filled learning curve moments involving the creation of our corporate profiles on various social media platforms. Similar to the rush to register web domain names in the late 90s, the current "land grab" is happening everywhere people and companies want—or may someday wish they had the foresight to secure—their own name on social platforms. This phenomenon will no doubt resonate with anyone who has tried to create a Gmail or Twitter account in their own name, only to receive the dialog box that says something like, "Sorry, that user name already exists, but 'schmidtjamison227usa2010' is still available!"

In our case, a panic kicked in when it occurred to our communications team that we should establish a LinkedIn group for SNUG (the Synopsys Users Group) only to discover that another entity had already set up a group profile with that name. Ouch! Who else would even want to do that, and how could they have thought about it before we did? And, oh by the way, how dare they!

There were several voices inside the company who expressed a knee-jerk impulse to try to shut down the group. After all, as the original founders of SNUG, didn't we own the *right* to administer a group with that name? Upon reflection, we realized that we don't actually need to try to own everything. Besides, one of the basic tenets of social media is that even if you want to own everything affiliated with your industry or company or brand, you simply can't. Remember our cheese analogy? You can't stop someone who is interested in starting a conversation about your cheese; you can only hope to join the conversation. So that's what we did.

Soon thereafter, we noticed one member of the SNUG group abusing his membership by posting frequent spam marketing messages. We sent an email message to the group administrator, introducing ourselves with a smile and an offer to help. The administrator responded by extending admin privileges to us, thereby initiating a collaborative partnership that has served this online community well. Today the SNUG group on LinkedIn is thriving with new requests for membership received almost daily from engineers throughout the world.

That experience had a ripple effect on the social media thinkers in the company. If we had already missed a land-grab opportunity in one social media space, where else was the name "Synopsys" being taken before we had a chance to show up at the party? A quick check on Facebook revealed that so far, no one had set up a fan page with our name, so, of course, we jumped! Then another social media oddity occurred: We soon found ourselves with over a hundred Facebook fans but no idea about what kind of content to post on the site. It was like a crowd of people had set up lawn chairs and laid out blankets in front of an outdoor stage, waiting for a concert to begin—and we, the headliners, didn't even have a set list. Now our Facebook page is populated weekly with events and stories from our employees and customers, but in those very early days, there wasn't a lot there.

This experience is an example of another phenomenon we've noticed on the social web: the impulse to associate—separate and distinct from any impulse to interact. Similar to the benign act of putting a decal on a car window from one's alma mater, the act of association can be an end unto itself. The people with Facebook accounts who joined the Synopsys fan page before there was any content or activity to interact with, for example, seemed sufficiently content to simply self-identify with the Synopsys logo.

The same is true for the aforementioned SNUG group on LinkedIn. Even though the group has over 1,100 members, there's very little discernable social interaction taking place. Why, then, do engineering geeks throughout the world take the time and initiative to join something they don't appear to actually use?

In part the answer, we believe, is explained by the propensity to self-associate with a logo or brand that reflects a valued attribute of oneself. Even though the Facebook platform is intrinsically social and the potential to socially interact is omnipresent, sometimes associating with an esteemed icon is utility enough.

By the way, the land grab phenomenon is not limited to company names and brands. The same is true among people, and it's spread across every new and blooming social media platform that crops up. Facebook and LinkedIn are obvious places to secure one's name, but what about Yammer or Plaxo or Google Buzz—or the next big thing that hasn't even crossed the radar screen yet? And what about those who aren't thinking about social media at all (yet), like a senior executive who might someday decide they need to jump into the social media sandbox and would be put out if their own name is no longer available?

As a result of this "What if?" game, we quietly but quickly established Twitter accounts on behalf of all our senior executives as placeholders against the day when (and if) they decide they want to join the Twittersphere. Good idea, but not soon enough to secure the preferred handle for our CEO, Aart de Geus. The best Twitter name available on the day we set up his account includes his middle initial ("J") because a Dutch politician with the same name got there first.

Because of the time we had invested in observing, listening, using, and thinking through other elements of the social media possibilities, we were able to grab the reins in these situations and work things out for the good of the company and the community. But wherever we were able to work from our plan, life was much calmer and a good deal less stressful.

Good planning requires clear thinking and thoughtful question asking. As valuable as the roadmap you're developing will be in guiding the implementation of your social media program, even more valuable is the process itself, if done to its fullest potential.

To achieve that potential, look at the planning process as a chance to better understand your company's culture. As an organization, do you truly believe that utilizing social media is a worthy endeavor? Or do you fundamentally think social media is a fad or a novelty that's only peripherally connected to your company's *real* business (the one that generates all the revenue)? What do your geek customers think about social media, and how likely are they to engage with your attempts to build an online community? What's the best possible outcome if your social media program is wildly successful? What aspects of social media are you worried about or downright afraid of?

Social media evangelists like to divide the world into those who "get it" and those who don't. Which camp do you suppose your CEO and CMO are in? How about your legal department, or Sales, or Support, or Marketing, or other members of the executive staff? Your boss?

Beyond all the clear thinking and thoughtful question asking, the planning process is ultimately an opportunity to seek alignment up and down the management chain as well as across the departments or business units that compose your organization. As such, your work in progress on *The Plan* is a tangible vehicle for the engagement, discovery, and consensus building that precedes meaningful action.

The Social Media Sandbox

One of the first things one notices when scoping out social media possibilities for the first time is the sheer abundance of tools, platforms, blogs, widgets, and fun colorful icons (one of the development stages in the life of many geeks is a fondness for cool-looking buttons and decals, so beware the siren call of their online equivalents).

If social media is a sandbox full of cool stuff to figure out and potentially adopt, how should a company think about the question "How should social media change our business goals?" The answer is generally: "*They shouldn't!*" The challenge with social media isn't about how to deploy shiny new tools. The challenge is to understand how such tools can support and add value to existing business objectives.

This can't be overstated. One of the biggest mistakes we've observed is corporate social media enthusiasts letting the "shiny dime" syndrome[9] drive what's possible (and fun, and new, and personally satisfying) while losing sight of The Big Picture: business profit. If you and your team constantly discipline yourselves to ask "How will this affect our business?" you'll find the alignment challenges up the management chain and across notoriously "difficult" departments much easier to navigate.

Based on that philosophical framework, it's easy to see that spending time trying to figure out a Facebook strategy in isolation, or how to influence customers with Twitter tweets, absent a clear plan, is heading down the wrong path. The right path is the one that selectively chooses social media capabilities that map back to and advance the organization's primary care-abouts.

As is the case with two-story outhouses and lime green stretch pants, just because you can doesn't mean you should. Bring a business lens into the social media sandbox with you and use it to evaluate what fits and what doesn't with regard to customer engagement, corporate brand, and company culture.

This point is validated by Forrester's "Rethinking The B2B Tech Marketing Mix In The Digital Age"[10] research, where Laura Ramos writes "With the exception of email and the corporate web site, most marketers say the majority of tactics they use fail to generate leads effectively. Less than one in five respondents said direct mail, forums, or online ads were very effective at boosting demand. All social media fared just as badly; roughly 20 percent of respondents who use them said blogs, social networks, and video helped to heighten awareness. These results continue to underscore the poor showing social media produces when marketers adopt the tools without understanding who the media will reach or how it will change relationships as buyers and sellers engage in community marketing."

Recipe for a Plan

As an organization alignment catalyst as well as a functional implementation roadmap, a social media plan should answer the questions "Where are we?" "Where do we want to go?" and "What steps will get us there?"

Your answers to "Where are we?" will form the basis for a traditional situation analysis, which not only describes the current landscape, but also adds insights and analysis that leads to a clearly articulated point of view. Given the sequence Landscape > Insights > Point of View, the description of the landscape should be as objective as possible. Think facts. What can you factually say about what your competitors and customers are doing in the social media space? Do they have a "Community" area on their corporate website and, if so, what facts can you describe about it (e.g., number of blogs, frequency of posts, level of customer engagement as measured by number of comments or forum threads and so on)? What else are they doing beyond the corporate website (e.g., Twitter activity, Facebook fan page, LinkedIn groups)? The aggregate of these and other fact-based observations will form a clear picture of the overall environment your social media program will exist within.

Once the landscape is accurately framed, the next step is to bring subjective insights and wisdom to form a picture with deeper meaning to your specific organization. This step is the analog to the previous step's digital. What can you say about the quality of what you've just described in the landscape? Where are your competitors strongest, and where are they missing the boat? What are the best opportunities for your organization to bring unique value into a wider environment that already exists?

The combination of your quantitative and qualitative assessments leads to the step where you plant a flag and declare a Point of View. This is the rallying point around which consensus needs to be built. It's the conclusion to "If A, and if B, then C." But, unlike elementary algebra, the answer "C" is infinitely variable and only partially related to A and B. In that sense, the concept of planting a flag may yield to the image of rearranging the placement of a piano in a room—first here and then there, maybe that way about six inches or maybe where you had it originally. It's all part of the process. And, it's all good if internal discussion among stakeholders leads to an action plan that can be implemented with confidence.

Once you've established where you are, the next step is to decide where you want to go. This is the strategic part of the planning process where mission, vision, and objectives are established. Ideally, the mission and vision statements can be derived directly from the work already completed in the Point of View section. It's potentially a short step from a point of view that states "Online interaction with our customers through social media can strengthen relationships, deepen trust, and provide valuable engagement and feedback" to a mission statement along the lines of "The purpose of our social media-related programs is to measurably enhance trust, increase participation, and reinforce the customer-focused attributes of our brand."

The vision part of the social media plan takes the Mission Statement one step further by addressing the question "What does that look like?" Mission statements tend to be abstract creatures a bit on the lofty side. The value of the vision statement is to help bring the plan down to earth, get real, and set the stage for the next step: Establishing "SMART" objectives: Specific, Measurable, Attainable, Relevant, and Time-bound.[11]

By now you may have noticed that the social media planning process resembles a funnel, proceeding steadily and relentlessly from the general to the specific. With mission, vision, and SMART objectives neatly defined, all work towards mapping out the implementation phase, consisting of tactics, resources, and measurement.

Tactics are what cumulatively fulfill the objectives. They answer the question, "What needs to happen to fulfill the goal?" and "What should we work on first?" Tactics should be reasonably high level and cover deliverables like "Establish a Facebook fan page," rather than morphing into red tape by becoming too granular. There's nothing wrong with keeping detailed to-do lists, but too much detail may dilute the value of the social media plan more than help it.

The resources section of the plan should cover the topics of people, tools, and budget. This section progresses from broadly asking "What will we need to get this done?" to specifically answering some nuts and bolts aspects of your program:

- "Who will do the work?"
- "What tools will they need to get it done?"
- "How much money is needed to pay for it all?"
- "How will we measure success?"

Finally, consider creating a company-wide social media policy as an integral part of your plan. We cover the specifics of how to do this in the next chapter, but for now, make sure in your strategic plan there's a place for the policy *and* a plan for how to make sure it gets distributed throughout your organization! Nobody gets off with "...but I didn't know we weren't supposed to mess around with a competitor's Wikipedia page!"

Adaptive Planning

Planning is important, even essential, but you can't cast your social media plan in stone. Staying responsive to changing conditions and new insights is integral to the long-term success of your program. And man, do the conditions change quickly online! Framing your social media plan as a living document that reflects your current best thinking—but is also open to change—provides the best of both worlds.

> **G2G is neither B2B nor B2C**
>
> My recent TEDx talk focused on G2G. G2G is not B2B, and it's not B2C. The social media techniques that are great for selling soda or office supplies simply do not work when you are marketing to geeks. The first word in Social Media Marketing is "Social." That's a problem when marketing to a demographic that tends to be asocial. The final word in Social Media Marketing is "Marketing." That's another gigantic challenge. Geeks do not like to be marketed to. At the first whiff of marketing, they're gone. You've lost all your credibility, broken your trust bond, and you may not get another chance. Prepare for the Twitter un-follows to pile up.
>
> Geeks really want technical information. They want to be able to find the technical information they need to do their job well. And they want to be able to find it quickly, and from a trusted source. That would be another geek, certainly not you, a marketer.
>
> Geeks are comfortable receiving technical information through the normal social media channels. If there is a good payback in technical information, geeks will hang out in Facebook groups, Twitter, forums, blogs, and the geeks' favorite social media tool, LinkedIn. They may not be there for the same purpose as your typical consumer, but they're there. They're looking for trusted technical information, and they're looking to get that information from a trusted source, someone like them—other geeks.
>
> *Rich Goldman*
> *VP, Corporate Marketing & Strategic Alliances*
> *Synopsys*

Chapter 5 Listen

Why Listen?

If you make it a practice to diligently monitor what's being said about your company on the web, that can put you ahead of what your competition is doing; regardless of who else is joining you in the practice, it's a very good idea. Why?

1. You want to know when someone says something amazingly good about your product/company/CEO/dragon boat team. It gives you a lovely glow that makes you look ten years younger, gives you a chance to pass along the good news to the appropriate parties inside your company, and alerts you to an opportunity to personally circle back to the source of the news with a note of community-building thanks.

2. You definitely want to be among the first to hear bad news so your company has a chance to proactively respond and/or begin damage control if necessary. Plus, being first on the scene gives you a shot at attaining "corporate hero" status.

3. You want to be able to relax amid the soothing white noise of nothing remarkable transpiring in cyberspace, good or bad. The fact is that most of the web-based mentions

about your brand fall into this category—news releases bouncing around the virtual echo chamber along with all manner of institutionally-generated background noise. Most web chatter initiated by actual geeks where brands are even mentioned tends to be entirely tame. Still, it's comforting to know when someone is talking about your company as you picture yourself on the banks of a river watching endless tidbits of insight float by—glimpses into who, what, when, where, why, and how people are talking about your cheese.

Although listening is a great idea for all these reasons, be aware that you're about to enter a world that can be unfamiliar to traditional marketers.

The traditional marketing paradigm that came of age with mass media was a thing of beauty—a golden era when advertisers got to control their message and maintain a steady drum beat of brand reinforcement limited only by budget and imagination. Sure, individual consumers talked and shared personal experiences with other individuals, but nobody had the reach or sphere of influence commanded by those who could afford the bully pulpit of I-tell/you-listen marketeers.

Then, along came the Internet. At first, the traditional marketing paradigm still applied as companies honed and polished corporate websites to present HTML versions of their brand, marketing slogans, and other controlled content. Shiny new guitar, but same old songs. All the while, the Internet was morphing into something bigger and more powerful than a collection of websites, one after another like so many billboards on the highway.

Social media make it possible for individuals to use the Internet to communicate with many—as many, in theory, as the total number of people on planet earth who are connected online. Though the heralding trumpets were heard clearly by few beyond the early adopters, the playing field was undeniably leveled in a way that enabled individuals to gain exposure, stature, and credibility as never before at the same time well-established brands began realizing that theirs were no longer the exclusive voices of influence.

Today it's well understood that conversations can and do take place on the Internet at any time—with you or without you—and neither your PR team, nor your best writers of corporate collateral, get to control the topic or the talk.

As many social media evangelists are fond of saying, "The community decides." That's why it's important to listen to what's being said about your brand online. Although total Internet traffic is measured in exabytes[12] (1 EB = 1,000,000,000,000,000,000 B = 1018 bytes = 1 billion gigabytes = 1 million terabytes[13]), none but a tiny fraction of all that chatter and other activity has anything at all to do with your company. Fortunately, there are tools available to help you systematically find the needles in endless haystacks without losing your marbles for the trouble.

Geeks Love the Intrawebs

They love sitting behind a computer writing code, testing a network server, reading about the latest gadget from Google Reader and of course tweeting and blogging along the way. They life their lives on the social web; it's in their DNA.

Geeks don't have egos. They don't care how many Twitter followers they have or if their own content gets re-tweeted. All they care about is content that interests them; and they have no problem talking about it all day and sharing that content within their social circles.

Geeks hate marketing. Most use browsers that hide any potential advertisements or pop ups, and I don't blame them. They probably even use or write scripts that automatically delete any tracking cookies on their browsers. And, it gets really bad when marketers try to push their one way messages to geeks in public, specifically Twitter. Not only will they get blocked, but they will get publicly scrutinized, belittled, and put in check for everyone to watch.

> Geeks are influencers, and that's why so many brands try to market to them. If brands truly want to engage with geeks, they need to speak their language and add value to the conversation. What this means is that they have to spend a substantial amount of time listening to the conversation. And then with real people, ideally other geeks (engineers) engage in a dialogue that adds value to the industry as a whole and not just the brand.
>
> **Michael Brito**
> **VP, Social Media**
> **Edelman Digital**

Systematic Listening

Systematic listening begins with the process of developing a list of keywords that you can instruct a software application to listen for on your behalf. Your list might include the name of your company, your top products, your key executives, and maybe the names of your competitors, or any other topic you're interested in monitoring. The trick is to land on a set of keywords that produce the results you're actually looking for, which is typically harder to accomplish than it would seem.

In the electronic design automation (EDA) industry, for example, the top three companies are Synopsys, Cadence Design Systems, and Mentor Graphics. The keyword "Synopsys" will deliver content related to Synopsys the company along with recaps of every TV show, book, or movie where somebody made a typo in "synopsis." The word "Cadence" is used in the context of music as much as EDA, "Mentor" will turn up all manner of teachers and "Design" and "Graphics" covers everything from crayons to Renaissance masterpieces. In such cases, stock symbols might help (but only in finding content that includes the correctly spelled symbols, which is bound to miss a wide swath of informal chatter). Trial and error are inevitable, but your best bet is to think in terms of standard search operators (e.g., Synopsys AND design).

If keywords are hooks, then search-based social media monitoring apps are the fishing rods needed to deliver the results you seek. Such apps are either free or not free. There are many companies that offer social media monitoring solutions. The granddaddy of them all is Google itself, although not necessarily the best choice for producing real-time results. This is because Google's proprietary algorithms favor content that earns its way to a high-ranking search result through longevity and other value-related criteria (spontaneous chatter is not particularly high on the list).

Some of the most popular free social media monitoring apps are Google Alerts and Twitter clients such as Tweetdeck, Seesmic, Twazzup, and HootSuite. Since an ever-growing number of niche conversations take place on Twitter, any software that can search for keywords in tweets can be used to monitor that increasingly important ocean of potentially relevant discourse.

Google Alerts are free email updates of the latest news results found by Google based on search criteria that you enter. The Google Alerts interface enables one to constrain searches to News, Blogs, Video, or Discussions (or Everything), specify the frequency of notification (once-a-day, once-a-week, or as-it-happens) and preview the results of any keyword parameters prior to creating an alert. Google Alerts are particularly useful for monitoring a developing news story or keeping current on a competitor or industry—or your own company.

Socialmention.com is a free social media search platform that aggregates user-generated content from across the web into a single search result. It works like a straight Google search but is optimized for social media sources, including Twitter, Facebook, FriendFeed, YouTube, and others.

Not to be overlooked: good ol' RSS (Really Simple Syndication). The primary purpose of an RSS feed is to alert you whenever something new is published anywhere you've established a subscription. Very powerful, but also very limited in that you have to know in advance which sources of content are worth monitoring. Even with a superb list of sources, RSS will do nothing to alert you to content posted anywhere you have not subscribed.

Free search, alerts, and RSS feeds are excellent resources to get started with social media monitoring. All are good at delivering raw results (often big heaping haystacks full of unsorted items) but offer a limited number of ways to categorize or further analyze the data. The best way for enterprises to take social media monitoring to the next level is to use a commercial tool.

"Such tools deal with the issues of gathering, categorizing, and analyzing online conversations," explains FreshMinds Research, a consultancy based in the UK. "They use web crawling technology similar to search engines in the way that they read online conversations. However, unlike search engines, the tools clean, de-duplicate and categorize the conversations and then store them in a database... some tools do this better than others."[14]

Getting to Know You

Once you select the social media monitoring tools that best meet your budget, ease of use, and other requirements, the next step is to tune into the buzz about your brand. The first time you listen is akin to scanning the dial on a ham radio: static ...more static ...and then life beyond anything you knew before.

Mixed in with more press releases than you can count, advice on which stocks to buy or dump, and encouraging signs that, yes, the job boards have plenty of openings for all walks of geek, you'll find the actual jewels you were hoping would be there. The more esoterically geeky your company, the fewer the likely number of jewels. By tracking relevant chatter through time, you'll see patterns emerge. Certain individuals are bound to have more to say than others. If they're credible, they have the potential to become opinion leaders in your space and are thus clearly worth reaching out to. Others may be blips on the radar screen and not particularly advantageous to elevate, especially if outreach bandwidth is scarce. For those in the middle ground, consider assessing credibility by looking at social capital in the form of Twitter followers, LinkedIn connections and other such indicators of engagement and influence.

On a macro level, some social media monitoring tools provide support for tracking sentiment about your brand, which can be a valuable barometer of perceptions in the market and useful in identifying possible trends.

What to Do with What You Hear

"What if they criticize us or say something bad?" That's often the greatest fear expressed by those entertaining the concept of social media for the first time. The reality is, however, that people will say whatever they're inclined to say, whether you're listening, whether you want them to, or whether you approve or not.

It's always better to know where there's trouble brewing than to be caught with your head in the sand. And from time to time, you might even score a bonus: Delivering great customer service has been known to generate positive comments about how well you resolved the source of the original issue.

Note that doing nothing is always an option. There is no social media rulebook that mandates a response to every comment, blog post, or tweet. The rule of thumb is to use the same judgment that applies to every other form of community engagement and respond appropriately wherever appropriate.

Beyond Listening

As implied earlier in this chapter, engagement is the companion of listening. At its core, "social media" is about relationship building, networking, developing trust networks, and all of the other things people do in "real life" to participate in—and therefore strengthen—communities.

Listening is a great first step towards meaningful engagement that's both welcome and appreciated within the community of which you are a part. Listen well, and good outcomes are bound to follow.

More Reasons to Monitor Your Brand in Cyberspace

Find Opinion Leaders

An opinion leader's posts (and audience) can help spread opinions on a brand quickly and with notable impact—good folks to make friends with

Gain Competitive Insights

Tapping into what your competitors are saying—and what's being said about them—is a valuable source of competitive intelligence, good or bad

Monitor for Pleas for Help

When someone uses their social media network to publicly ask for help (e.g., to solve a problem, make a purchase decision), consider reaching out with an offer of assistance

Listen to the Wisdom of Crowds

Following the tide of trending topics can help uncover topics and discussions you may want to keep tabs on

Track Engagement

Tracking the mentions of a brand in user-generated content before, during, and after a marketing campaign can yield useful insights about the effectiveness of the initiative

Find the Sweet Spots

Identifying which sites are discussing your brand can help pinpoint possible ad or article placement opportunities to reach the most valuable and engaged audiences

Stitch Together Threads

Using keywords to follow discussions that migrate from site to site can help bridge fragmented conversation threads for easier analysis

Locate Points of Entry

People are chatting about your brand, industry, and competitors online right now, with or without you. Listen—and look for opportunities to join the conversation

---

It's not you, it's ...well, it *is* you.

I often hear that geeks just aren't into social media; or they're too shy to participate for whatever reason. What I've found is wrapped up in one of my favorite jokes:

A 7 year-old boy, who has never uttered a word in his short life, is sitting at dinner eating a bowl of succotash—something new his mother was trying out. The boy looks up after swallowing a mouthful.

"I hate succotash," he says clearly and succinctly.

His parents are stunned. His mother cries in joy and his father exclaims, "You talked!"

"So?" the boy replies.

"But you've never said anything before."

The boy looks down at his bowl, then at his mother, and then says to his father: "Up to now, everything has been OK."

I think it is an adequate description of how hardware geeks approach social media.

When things are going well, geeks keep their heads down and work. When things go wrong, they bitch and moan to each other as they try to resolve the problem. If you don't have an answer for them, then stay out of the conversation.

Hardware geeks will use social media to find answers to a problem, and they will engage in productive conversation. But, they won't put much effort into useless discussion.

So when the people running a social media program don't get much engagement from their audience, it may not be because the engineers are shy. It may just be that there is nothing worth talking about.

Lou Covey
Blogger, State of the Media
President, Footwasher Media

Chapter 6
Talk

In the world of geek-to-geek social media as in the rest of life, talking takes many forms and is almost always context-dependent. Consider the differences in substance, formality, and tone between peers talking shop in a break room, technology experts sharing knowledge in a conference, collaborators updating status in a meeting, and families passing the time at the dinner table. All talk-conducive contexts, and all quite different.

On the web, context ranges from the informality and transience of a personal Twitter or Facebook account to the flexibility and immediacy of a forum comment to the structure and enduring presence of a wiki or company-hosted blog. Maybe the biggest difference between cyberspace and the physical world is that, in the former, everything one says instantly becomes a matter of public record bound for a digital life all its own.

If you're a blogger, that may be your greatest hope—to reach an audience greater than one. But, in other situations, be aware that email messages, Facebook updates, Twitter tweets, Yelp reviews, forum comments—literally any and every form of digital communication—has the potential to live well beyond its intended life (or audience).

As long as you exercise the same discretion and good judgment online as you do in other parts of your personal and professional life, no worries. A good rule of thumb: Remind yourself that once you hit the Enter key, you will have zero control over the future of your communication. If there's no inner voice urging caution regarding that which you're about to send, you should be just fine.

Why Blog?

Blogs build credibility—for the blogger, your company, and your brand. Credibility is currency, and that's always good to have. Blogs also build community by engaging others with shared interests. Search engines love blogs for their fresh new content flavor. The anticipation of a fresh post will give people a reason to return to your website. They contribute to thought leadership, and in some cases, can even help your company completely rethink a topic.

Blogging Geek-To-Geek

In the minds of many, the most prestigious form of online talk is the *Blog*. A blog (short for "web log") is a journal-style website (or part of a website):

- Written in the first person with a conversational voice

- Published at a reliable interval and updated frequently with content that's valuable to its readers

- Reader interaction encouraged

A well-executed blog can set the author apart as an expert in his or her field, which can be both career-enhancing for the blogger and leadership-strengthening for the sponsoring company and brand. Blogging can build and strengthen networks and position in the community for individuals and their employers alike, especially for those who remember that a blog is a valuable community relationship—much more than just a publishing platform.

Corporate Bloggers

So where does one recruit corporate bloggers? Within geek cultures, you look for subject-matter experts who have both an interest and the ability to write engaging material, *and* who are socially inclined to interact with others on their topic. This includes not only responding to comments received on their own blog, but also actively participating in related online venues.

In part, it's a temperament thing. At its best, blogging is talking aimed at social interaction, and as we'll see in following chapter, the blogger should be passionate about their topic *and* be motivated to engage in their community of readers at a level that buffs the sheen on your corporate brand. Even for those who meet the basic criteria, it's one thing to like the idea of blogging and another thing altogether to truly enjoy the week-in/week-out *work* that's required to begin and maintain a successful blog.

Thus, not every expert is a good candidate to be a blogger. Not every writer is a good candidate to be a blogger, either. Unless the writer is at least a moderately social critter by inclination and passionate about his or her subject, the level of interaction a successful blog requires may prove to be too demanding for long-term sustainability.

It's also essential to have support from the blogger's management chain and to anticipate what insights and data points might be needed to garner said support.

How much time will blogging take, and on whose time?

Depending on the blogger and their customary post length, use of photos, and so on, a reasonable starting spot will be a minimum of one to three hours per post, and one post per week. The question of "on whose time?" is a little more tricky to address.

Even if an employee declares that they don't care if they get time to write during work hours and are willing to do it in their free time, employers have been known to decline the offer. The thinking behind their negative response can run a number of different paths.

They may be genuinely concerned about their employees "life balance" and would prefer they use time off to really step away from work-related functions and just decompress and refresh themselves. They may have concerns about intellectual property ownership issues down the road if the work was done "off the clock." They might have customer confidentiality or transparency or loss-of-control concerns. Or they might just be over-saturated with the relentless barrage of "new media" opportunities that they can't keep up with. There are many reasons a manager might not be willing to support the idea of an employee blogging. So if, after your best attempts to understand and mitigate the concerns, you still get a red light on blogging, give it up.

Nobody can be a successful blogger while under a cloud of possibly taking "too much time" on their blog at the expense of getting "real" work done. If the boss hands down an emphatic "no," neither you nor your potential blogger should waste time arguing the point. The challenges ahead are hard enough for a blogger without also having to worry about getting bitten from behind.

By now, it should be clear that bloggers shouldn't launch until their eyes are wide open regarding the level of commitment involved. A blog becomes like a family pet that still needs to be fed, watered, groomed, played with, and walked well after the endearing puppy stage has ended.

Perhaps now you understand why there are relatively few "star" technology bloggers, and why it's imperative to approach the building of a corporate stable of bloggers with enthusiasm *and* realistic expectations, both for their sakes—and yours!

Why I Blog

I have been blogging for several years, and so far what I've learned is that people seem to be appreciative of honest opinion and don't seem to mind if my opinion doesn't match their expectations. Some engineers don't seem to like my blog, as most of my topics are pretty dry, and it has no humor—probably because of my nature and that I'm not good at cracking technical jokes!

Most of the engineers who read my blog seem to read or subscribe because it is:

   a. Very technical
   b. Focused on a current "hot-topic:" low power
   c. Inclusive of topics from verification?implementation?sign-off, etc.
   d. Not biased towards any EDA vendor
   e. Not marketing information
   f. Expressed in engineering language!

I often discuss interesting ideas with various engineers. Before I started blogging, those discussions stopped there and only included one set of engineers. By blogging I can share ideas with a much bigger audience. When I see the interest level among engineers asking various questions based on a certain topic, it motivates me to continue discussing those subjects. Plus, I like that there is no time limit as compared to having a discussion with a particular person.

I have tons of topics to blog on but often don't find time to do it. If I look back to the beginning, I was originally hesitant to blog. Now I enjoy blogging and am quite passionate about it.

Godwin Maben
Corporate Application Engineer and Synopsys Blogger
"Magic Blue Smoke"[15]

Creating a Successful Blogger

Your bloggers will need a primary go-to person for blog-related issues and education. Chances are, if you're still reading this, that person is you. They'll have questions about the blogging platform you've chosen: How do they post a photo or a video or an audio file? They'll need a heads up on the latest plug-ins that are available and how to use them, not to mention the etiquette, style, and other "softer" aspects of blogging. Shocking as this may seem, there may be occasions that demand an intermediary between the bloggers and the web team. Your bloggers will be looking for someone to provide metrics, feedback, and meaningful analysis, and to share social media insights in the ever-changing landscape. They might need help with search engine optimization practices to improve the discoverability of their content. Having someone around to provide general support and encouragement, and to dispense the inevitable bird-dogging that's sometimes necessary when too many priorities collide can mean the difference between a successful blog and one that withers and dies on the vine.

When you consider that maintaining the frequency of posts is a challenge for most bloggers, it's not surprising that an online community manager can make a huge difference by just checking in to see if things are okay and if there's anything he or she can do to help when a blogger is going through a dry spell. Similarly, an editorial calendar can be a great mechanism for creating structure and accountability in the blogging stables.

Who Owns the Content?

If someone is a gifted writer of code and writes something brilliant during the course of his or her workday, who owns the code? The company does, of course, and it will go to great lengths to keep that "work product" protected, confidential, and closely held. The inverse logic regarding work product applies, however, in the social media space.

A blog, by default, is intended to be distributed across as wide an audience as possible, and the more links, mentions, references, quoted passages, and other forms of social media echoes, the stronger the blog becomes. As long as credit is attributed to the original source, a blog post is like corporate compost: the thicker and wider the material is spread around, the better. For this reason, we find the whole question of content ownership somewhat antithetical in this domain.

Yes, a blog that's created during work hours while you're in the employment of a company is, by default, work property. And while the blogger may be personally invested in the content, the copyright owner of record is clearly the employer. However, technology companies should recognize that blogs are not their primary business, so what's to be gained by taking a hard line on bloggers quoting themselves in other places, for example, their own personal blogs.

After all, copyright law provides for "fair use" where attribution is cited and no money is changing hands, so who wants to get into a push-and-shove over the nickels and dimes of content that's specifically designed to be spread as far and wide as possible? Bottom line: No harm, no foul.

When Bloggers Move On

At some point, companies face inevitable moments when a blogger decides (or gets decided upon) to leave the company. What then about the blogger's published works?

We believe that the best idea is to let the blog live on. Your company has invested corporate dollars on the hours it took to develop the content. From a corporate perspective, the content is intellectual property and thus an asset. Blogs have followers, and followers are assets too. Blog content is also valuable from a search engine optimization (SEO) perspective, because it can drive traffic to your site through organic search. But how to move forward when the writer is no longer there?

We believe it's a fair practice to permit another employee to take over the blog when the original blogger leaves. Geek-authored corporate blogs are almost always centered on a technology topic and thus are more content-driven than personality-driven. That's not to say, of course, that an individual's personality and voice don't factor into the blog. On the contrary, blogs without personality are essentially white papers without kennel club certification. But since a geek blog is almost always about technology, first and foremost, the "long tail" of information, insights, opinion, questions, and comments has long-term value for the company. So, while it may take a while to transition the current readership to a new voice, the topic itself is likely to sustain enough readership interest to weather the change in tide.

Also, it's important not to remove the published posts of the former employee. Let the content live in the archives while giving the new blogger the freedom to bring their own perspectives to the conversation.

Creating a Successful Blog

So how does one go about creating a successful blog? Here are five basic recommendations:

Establish a Clear Scope

What's the scope and general theme of your blog? This consideration may seem obvious, but thinking it through before launching a new blog is an important first step. Developing an outline of topics you'd like to cover can be helpful in narrowing your focus as well as building an initial pipeline of ideas to draw from down the road.

Be Consistent

New posts keep subscribers coming back, and they add juice to search engine indexes. Frequency recommendation: Weekly is optimal (not counting time invested interacting with reader comments). Every other week is OK. More often than that is hard to sustain (for author and reader alike), and a lesser frequency tends to lose traction.

Keep it Simple

As every writer knows, the space between staring at a blank screen and finding the groove that begins with the first few keystrokes can be daunting at times. The good news is that you're blogging, not writing the next great novel. Keep your blog posts simple, single-topic focused, and not too lengthy, and your readers are likely to appreciate your communication style. Plus, writing blog posts is apt to become as natural as tapping out email messages—a skill you've long ago mastered completely.

Think Links

Building *inbound* links is a priority for most bloggers, and for good reason: They drive click-through traffic from other blogs, they increase your exposure around the blogosphere, and they help to boost your search engine rankings. Getting a few links from respected blogs can help with search engine traffic, but the added credibility that you get can be just as important, especially for newer bloggers. The way to start here, by the way, is to link to *their* blogs first. Even highly successful bloggers are interested in the people and blogs who are sending traffic their way and often surprise and delight a newbie blogger with a kind comment of thanks and appreciation.

Have Patience

New blogs generally take a minimum of several months before they gain enough trust from search engines to produce any type of significant flow of traffic. Building a blog that's search engine-friendly is critical if you want to maximize search traffic, so take care of that from the start and focus on creating great content that others will talk about and link to. In addition, although posting needs to be consistent to keep traffic levels up, that doesn't mean that traffic levels will always be consistent. Every blog has ups and downs—be sure that you enjoy the times when traffic is high, and keep on plugging away to get through the slower times.

Watch Your Tone

Some research suggests that brands may have to actually work a little harder than individuals to build and maintain trust and credibility in online communities. According to a recent IDC study, "Web 2.0 is accelerating the need for the marketer to become a trusted educator. Through social networks, buyers increasingly learn from each other as well as vendors. The information transfer is immediate, more trusted (though not always more trustworthy), and very relevant.

"For vendors to have a voice in a purchase-related conversation that is increasingly becoming peer to peer, they need to participate in the conversation with the level of credibility and relevance a buyer expects from a peer community. However, vendors at large have a credibility issue they must overcome. When IDC asked buyers, 'Who are the participants in your ideal online community?' respondents ranked vendors far below peers and independent authorities."

Given such sentiment, corporate bloggers will do well to err on the side of being overly humble, and not overly arrogant.

Ideas for Blog Topics

Everyone who blogs has a problem—if not today, then eventually.

The problem: figuring out what to write about when you can't think of any good topics. It's one of those stare-at-a-blank-canvas things. You know you need to post something new, but what do you do when the well is dry?

It's not a rhetorical question. Once a blog is launched, bloggers have an obligation to continue blogging at regular intervals. Those who don't (or can't) keep pace are predictably destined to experience the vision that originally inspired them going nowhere.

Content is king in the blogosphere, so if you're not creating new content on a regular basis, you have a problem. But not to worry: Help is at hand. The following are some tips on how to regularly drum up fresh fodder.

Teach

You have insights and experience locked up inside your brain that people are interested in knowing. You are an expert in your blog topic—use your blog as a platform to educate, teach and inform.

Lists

People love lists. Putting together a list of five, ten, or any defined number is a great way to share your expertise, but do it in a concise and clear way.

Links

Finding good content on the web isn't always as simple as it appears to be. People will appreciate it if you make it easy for them by making a list of links to good content.

Experience

Storytelling is an art form. It's also an extremely effective way of making a point. Telling the first-hand story of an interesting challenge is top-notch fodder for a blog post.

Book Reviews

Read a good book about your topic and write a review on it. Make it easy for your readers to find the book by providing links to Amazon.com or other online resources.

Answer Questions

People are always asking questions about your expertise and/or your product, so why not answer those questions in the form of an FAQ (Frequently Asked Questions) that can also be used as a reference resource to send people to later?

Comment on Other Blogs

Commenting on blogs is a great way to build presence, but sometimes a comment becomes too good to simply leave on another site. Turn it into a blog post on your site that links back to the original discussion and then expands upon the original article.

Check Your Email

We all are on email overload. Is there any way that you can turn some of this information—either correspondence that you've cleared with the sender or information you received—into a blog post to share with a wider audience?

Write For The Noobs

Explain something about your subject that might be confusing to newbies. This is the type of information that people could be searching for, and they just might find your site when they do the search.

Case Studies

The real-life application of principles is always illustrative and helpful.

Conduct a Poll

Polls can be good for multiple blog posts. Present the objective and questions in one blog post, and follow up later with the results and analysis.

It Starts with a Connection

Engineers like to sit in their offices, make plans, and create well-defined tasks to execute. I've noticed a difference between "Geeks" and technical people, "Engineers." True "Geeks" get connected. Geeks buy new stuff, like iPhones. Engineers often go for good enough. Their phones make phone calls. Maybe Engineers get a Facebook account to monitor their kid. The engineer expands Facebook to old friends, Geek Friends. (Sometimes Facebook connects Engineers to old flames.) Facebook converts the Engineer to the Geek (or part way there). My point: You need a hook to use social media to bring in the Engineers, and transform them into Geeks. It starts with a connection. How do you do that?

You need to get in front of them. You need to meet them. Show them you have value in person. Connect. Connect physically, then virtually. It's slow. It's arduous. You can break headline news, but I'm not that guy, and I'm betting you aren't either. You must create value, link ideas, show creativity. If you can do it in person, you can bring Engineers to your virtual environment with social media.

> Make your Engineers more like Geeks. Create a social media center point for your business to focus on, to point to. You can create a Blog, a URL, a Facebook page, a Twitter feed, a podcast, your Ping, (or what comes after Facebook) that you can point all your social media to. You can augment all your other marketing efforts. But it's *social*. It must contain your character. Connect with your Engineers. Commit to social engineering all your Engineers to build your own Social Media Geek empire.
>
> *Eric Huang*
> *Product Marketing Manager and Synopsys Blogger*
> *"To USB or Not to USB"*

Executive Blogging

Every organization that successfully launches a blog will inevitably one day ask itself, "Should our CEO blog?"

Many business decisions have an obvious answer. Should we generate more revenue? (Yes) Should we increase shareholder value? (Yes) Should we give away all of our products and services for free? (No) Some decisions, however, involve multiple trade-offs where answers are not immediately obvious, but optimized against a range of complex considerations. The question of executive blogging falls squarely into this category.

A study conducted by ÜBERCEO in 2009[16] found that "the top CEOs in the country appear to be mostly absent from the social media community." The study looked at Fortune's 2009 list of the top 100 CEOs to determine how many have blogs or use Twitter, Facebook, or LinkedIn. Here are the top-line results:

- Not one Fortune 100 CEO had a blog

- Only two CEOs had a Twitter account

- Thirteen CEOs had LinkedIn profiles; of those, only three had more than ten connections

Forrester analyst Laura Ramos noted in "How to Derive Value from B2B Blogging" (June 2008) that "Business-to-business (B2B) marketers find it difficult to publish a corporate blog that consistently attracts readers and engages them in conversation. Forrester reviewed 90 company blogs from Fortune 500 and leading technology firms ... and were disappointed to find that:

1. corporate bloggers struggle to sustain a conversation,
2. blogs read like tired, warmed-over press releases and
3. user experiences are simply awful."

That's not to imply that there are zero CEO blogs. The roster, although not lengthy, includes J. Willard Marriott Jr., CEO at Marriott International, Mike Critelli, Executive Chairman at Pitney Bowes, and Colin Byrne, CEO at Weber Shandwick, to name a but a few.

The question remains: What about *your* CEO? In addition to all the factors that apply to corporate bloggers in general (see above), there are some key questions you'll need to address before making a recommendation one way or the other:

- Why establish an executive blog? (What's the objective?)
- What difference would it make?
- Will it result in increased business?
- Would having your CEO blog result in gaining new customers?
- Would not having your CEO blog result in losing existing customers?
- What's the value proposition?
  - For shareholders
  - For customers
  - For employees
- What are the potential benefits?
  - Thought leadership?

- Platform for crisis communications?
- Connection with social media-aware constituencies?
- Public insight into how the company thinks?

- What are the potential risks?
  - Legal obligations of company officers
  - Wall Street
  - Inconclusive business case (questionable or difficult to justify ROI)
- How will we measure success?
- What's the best format? (e.g., blog, video)
- Engagement model: What are the community's expectations?
- What's the workflow? (including, how much executive bandwidth would be needed?)
- What's the review/approval process? (PR, IR, etc.)

Adding Video to a Blog

The research conducted by the students at Santa Clara University (referenced in the Introduction) revealed that a majority of the engineering geeks surveyed are interested in and receptive to YouTube-style video content. Compared to the relatively low numbers reported for numerous other social media options, nearly two-thirds of the SNUG and DesignCon audiences indicated that they use YouTube on a regular basis, and a substantial majority finds video to be a particularly valuable means of learning new information. This means a good video is a great option to include in your corporate blogs. Note: *good* video is a great option. Crappy video that has an inaudible sound track, where it's impossible to see who is talking, or that's so jerky that it looks like it was shot by someone with hiccups—not such a great option. So put on the popcorn as we set the stage with the following video production tips:

- When shooting on location, be aware of the background behind your subject. Are there visual distractions that can be eliminated or improved with a different camera angle?

- Avoid strong backlights—place your subject against as dark a background as possible with primary lighting illuminating the subject from the front

- The backlight should not be stronger than the primary light source

- Use a tripod whenever possible

- When panning a wide area, hold the camera in the palm of your hand as you slowly scan the field of view—this method minimizes the jitters often evident in hand-held video

- Position the camera such that your subject's eyes are one-third of the way down from the top of the screen. If possible, have your subject stand. People tend to be less stiff, more animated and consequently more "real" when they have their whole body in the conversation

- Positioning the camera at eye level also minimizes foreshortening or parallax-related issues that cannot be fixed in post-production

- Be aware of background noise. Wind, cutlery against plates, traffic, background conversations, even air conditioning can wreck what could otherwise be a perfect video shoot. If necessary, move your subject to a more quiet location before you start the shoot (unless the ambient noise is helpful to lend credibility to location shots)

- Leave some recording "head" and "tail" room for editing purposes. This means record for a couple of seconds before silently nodding your head that they can begin to talk, and then let the camera roll for another few seconds at the end of their sentence

- Avoid providing verbal feedback until the camera is shut off. (Yes, that seems intuitively obvious but oddly difficult to remember at the time you are actually shooting.) All this makes things *much* easier for the folks doing the post-production work

- Begin with the end in mind: What do you want the viewer to do/think/believe as a result of spending one to three minutes with your subject? Make sure you get that message out front, early in the footage and then repeat it at the end

- Coax your speaker into using simple, natural, no-jargon English. This helps to ensure that your message is clearly understood

- For speakers who insist on a script or speaking notes, encourage them to try at least one run-through without cue cards or prompts. They will be surprised at how much they remember, and it might actually give the post-production folks some great natural footage to work with

Take a Test Drive

Working out the kinks when nobody's looking can make the difference between "No big deal" and "Wow that was embarrassing!" The most common form of a test drive is a development server. Such an environment simulates your social media infrastructure on a fully functional website but is not open for public view and scrutiny. Development servers are routinely used by web developers to test and interact with their work in progress, but can also be used by bloggers, editors and others who are responsible for web content.

Try embedding a YouTube video within the body of a blog post before officially launching the blog. Enlist the help of other team members to submit comments, subscribe to a blog with an RSS feed, or test the navigation of your site while it's still in the development environment.

In addition, since you're already working with geeks within your own company, don't overlook the opportunity to test concepts internally. This can be as simple as an informal conversation with a colleague down the hall or as orchestrated as a formal user acceptance testing (UAT) process.

What You Can Do with a Simple Point-and-Shoot Camera

Yes, we know that geeks are analytical, logical, and precise. They get pleasure from delving into the fine details of a product specification and they relish reading and analyzing datasheets and catalogues before they buy any product. For a geek, reading the feeds and speeds of the latest flat-screen TV is as delicious as eating a homemade, incredibly moist chocolate fudge cake iced with a delicate sour cream chocolate frosting with an added subtle hint of cinnamon and spice. BTW, my TV supports 1080p and 120 Hz, has a response time of 4 ms and a contrast ratio of 1:150,000. How about yours?

That's what geeks like. But let me tell you what they hate. Geeks abhor (literally) any slick, fluffy, corporate-generated marketing material. Those empty, meaningless messages describing how groovy a product is and how it will save 36 percent of your cost and at the same time will instantly increase your productivity by 25 percent. Go ahead and buy it now, because for every minute you are not using it, you are missing out on great saving opportunities. So, here is a test: Is it a good idea to bring in the media agency we used last year to generate a corporate video about our new industrial controller? Their last video was slick and flawless and right-on message.

Geeks have a huge tolerance for early product problems as long as they like the premise of its spec, and they have a special talent to work around bugs or clumsy user interfaces. Product bugs enable them to feel connected to the raw power of innovation—to the bleeding edge.

So, geeks hate slickness and love raw innovation coming right from the source. Got it?

As a former VP of Corporate Marketing who sold to geeks, my advice to you is: Pick up your point-and-shoot camera, stand behind the back of your best product manager, and ask him/her to talk passionately about the product. Don't edit the result. Leave it raw. You will get an authentic clip that sounds like a raw product spec and, to the geek, tastes like homemade chocolate cake.

Guri Stark
Chief Executive Officer
CloudShare

Chapter 7
Interact

Beyond "All About You"

The abilities to talk as well as listen online are defining characteristics of today's Internet, but it's the ability to engage and interact that makes the Internet social. The power of the Internet and the tsunami of social media are opening new doors and opportunities as they present compelling challenges for how to effectively communicate with customers. With community interaction at the core, welcome to the era of "Engage and Influence through Interaction."

Web 2.0 = two-way communication. Social media is the democratization of information, transforming people from content consumers (one-way communication) into members of online communities who are empowered to converse and participate with one another (multi-directional communication). As we've been hammering all along, social media shifts the marketing paradigm from "Tell Your Audience" to an "Engage and Participate" model rooted in conversations between content creators and community members.

It's interesting at this point to revisit the basic premise of "online community," with a special focus this time on the verbs involved. Note how several prominent bloggers define the term:

> "An online community is where a group of people with similar goals or interests connect and exchange information using web tools." (*Jeremiah Owyang, Web Strategist*)[17]

> "A community is a group of people who form relationships over time by interacting regularly around shared experiences, which are of interest to all of them for varying individual reasons." (*Mack Collier, The Viral Garden*)[18]

> "Communities are bodies of people loosely joined together by a common interest." (*Shel Israel, Global Neighborhood*)[19]

Note the common theme that emerges through words and phrases like "connect," "exchange information," "form relationships," and "interact." It's all about the movement of ideas, opinions, and information. And when that flow is vigorous, relevant, and shared by multiple participants, it can create the same exhilarating rush that's brought on by a great dinner party of animated conversationalists, punctuated with insights, laughter, and an experience of delightful camaraderie that makes everyone at the table feel privileged to be included. It's that sensation of inclusion and acceptance that's so addictive to those who gravitate to and enjoy social media.

"Social Media Works"

Skeptics may say that social media isn't useful for working with engineers, i.e., geeks. My experiences have shown quite the opposite.

One day, I was listening to what people were saying about my company (as I often do) on Twitter, when up popped a tweet that said our products suck. A traditional approach to the situation could have been to ask the person to retract the statement, issue a press release about how great our products are, tweet a denial to discredit the person, or hope that the person's tweet wouldn't be noticed. Instead, I decided to engage—geek-to-geek—with our customer.

I began following him, and he followed me back. Now I could approach him via direct message in a non-threatening way and find out why he said what he did. My direct message said something along the lines of, "Hi. I'm with Synopsys. Is there something I can do to help you?" Turns out, he was just venting about something that went wrong that day and everything was actually OK.

We continued to converse on Twitter, both publicly and privately. Eventually, he saw one of my tweets that invited people to join a committee that I was a member of. Unbeknownst to me, he'd been interested in participating in this area of work, and he signed up immediately. Had it not been for Twitter, I never would have met nor developed a working relationship with my customer.

I have two Facebook accounts, a public one for friends and activities and a private one for my family. With my public persona, I friended a fellow geek whom I'd worked with on a couple of projects. To my surprise, several of his friends began saying "Happy Birthday" to him—on *my* birthday! Because of Facebook and friending a fellow geek, we found out that we share a special day. Knowing personal aspects of people I work with seems to make our projects go smoother and without the tension that strangers have.

LinkedIn has become much more than an online Rolodex for me. (OK, kids, if you don't know what a Rolodex is, ask your mom or dad.) There is a growing community of bloggers in my field who enjoy learning from each other. We wanted a way to connect on an ongoing basis instead of once a year at our industry's annual conference. We experimented with some online communication tools and settled on a LinkedIn group as a good way to share information and meet new bloggers. Our group is active and enables us to continue working together to improve our blogging and visibility in our industry.

> I've had many experiences like this through Twitter, Facebook, and LinkedIn that prove that social media does indeed work for engaging geek-to-geek. At my company, those of us who use social media in our everyday work know that it makes real-world differences again and again.
>
> *Karen Bartleson, Sr. Director Community Marketing, Synopsys;*
> *author of The Ten Commandments for Effective Standards;*
> *blogger for "The Standards Game"*[20]

If you want your company to have a meaningful presence within that fabric, guess what? You need to offer exactly the same kind of support that's demanded of good conversationalists at the dining table: Take your turn to talk, but once you're done, don't just get up from the table and leave. Stick around and add your laughter, side notes, tangents, and expansions to keep the discussion alive: Participate!

A key part of the job ahead is to understand how the communities that are important to your organization want to be communicated with as social media becomes omnipresent. Where do your customers tend to congregate online? What sources do they trust and view as credible? How can you best serve their information needs without stepping over the line by whipping up a lather of marketing fluff?

Style is Everything

OK, so maybe style isn't actually everything, but it is a defining characteristic of corporate brand, and that introduces some interesting considerations in the realm of social media. As a brand, how does your company want to be seen by customers, employees, investors, analysts, competitors, and everyone else in the "community?" What's your corporate Twitter style? Your corporate marketing style? Your corporate social media style?

As you begin talking—whether through microblogs, comments, or a full-blown blog site—it's useful to reflect on how the personality and character of that talk meshes with the style and attributes of your brand and community. And if you're in a community populated by geeks, style counts just as much as it does anywhere else—if not more!

Think back to your observations in various corners where you found geeks lurking: Chances are there weren't a lot of instances of the words "yummy!" or "big hugs" or even "LOL" (though there may be many acronyms of the technical variety). Geek chatter tends to be direct, informative, technically focused, and occasionally witty or edgy. It is *not* peppered with smiley faces, gushy pronouncements celebrating minor family successes, cranky rants about traffic en route to the office, or personal revelations about loneliness, hormonal stress, or favorite chocolate chip cookie recipes. That's not to say you can't share your own perspective by relating personal experiences; it's just that the subject matter needs to stick to the topic at hand: geek stuff.

Prepare To Banter

Have you ever been cornered at a social mixer by a boorish so-and-so whose single topic of apparent interest is themself? In the real world, not the one you want to get stuck with at the dinner table. On the web, it's so easy to click away from boorish discourse that it's a non-issue. The real issue is ensuring that you don't become the one that others begin clicking away from.

The remedy to avoid being avoided? The give-and-take of two-way conversation. If you're a blogger, try asking a question at the end of a blog post or offering a thoughtful comment on another blogger's site. Anything you can do to reach out and stimulate dialog and interaction is a step in the right direction.

Pass the Word

Sometimes all it takes to engage and interact is to re-broadcast and attribute a bit of interesting content to your own social network. Analogous to the bridge card-table quip "Keep asking what's trump—it shows interest in the game," linking to content posted by other people is a high compliment to the original source that shows interest in your online community.

If you're a blogger, providing hyperlinks to relevant sources within a blog post both enriches the value of your own content (through cross-references) and does a favor for the linked sites (inbound links are among the factors Google uses to assess credibility, which is ultimately reflected in search ranking).

Comments Please?

Another form of online talk is the discourse that takes place on blogs and forums. In fact, the size of the community of commenters of a blog is considered an important metric in gauging the popularity of a blog or forum. One person makes a statement or asks a question, and others contribute their thoughts to the topic through threaded comments. (Threaded, or "nested," comments enable users who follow or engage in online discussions to easily keep track of who's saying what to whom.)

Like microblogging,[21] every comment posted on a blog or forum can contribute to one's virtual persona, an asset that has the potential to accrue social capital in the form of trust, authority, respect, credibility, etc.—which can lead to followers and an expanding sphere of influence.

Comments are a surefire way to build community on the web. Every blogger appreciates them (craves them actually), and every forum moderator knows that comments are the lifeblood that keeps any discussion alive. According to the "90-9-1" rule,[22] 90 percent of the participants in any online community quietly and anonymously engage with content in the background, 9 percent occasionally post a comment, and 1 percent account for almost all the discourse.

The math is clear: The act of commenting automatically distinguishes one from the pack. If your social media plan intends to accomplish that, then commenting is essential. Posting smart, thoughtful, insightful comments online is nothing less than an opportunity to share what you know, ask a question of your own, express an opinion, and otherwise add your unique voice to the conversations that form the social web.

Comments Anyone?

A client of mine is struggling to make sense of the growing number of blog posts by anybody and everybody. Is all this writing and blogging serving a real purpose? I'm not sure. Some blogs get recognition and response. I think most don't.

I think bloggers (indie, company, and editorial) all feel, in our gut, that there's value. But how do we measure that value? What do comments add to a blog or article? Tough one.

So I asked some well-known bloggers what they think. Here are some recurring points:

- The honeymoon infatuation period for EDA blogging has come, and is going. Now there needs to be some sense of long-term value. My take: "value" means different things from the client, journalist, and PR perspectives.

- Some indie bloggers say they see their blogs as diaries, written for themselves and interested people. My take: Everyone is aware of a larger cast of potential viewers. Few, however, look at comments as a metric of their blog's value.

- There are more eyeballs on blogs than we can ascertain. My take: this may be true, especially since it's impossible to get metrics for blogs one doesn't host.

- By and large, engineers are quiet, shy types who rarely will comment or extend a discussion even if they do read a blog. My take: this came up a lot.

- The number of comments isn't an accurate measure of eyeballs. My take: lots of agreement that some sort of metric on value is reasonable, but less agreement on whether it's actually helpful. One person compared the dilemma to the old attempt to equate value to column inches, which measures volume but doesn't take into account qualitative value.

- A blog and its comments, to some degree, form a community unto itself. My take: This discussion got a bit abstract for me but I hear the notion. Help!

- Everyone thought we ought to keep talking about this issue. My take: Comments anyone?

Ed Lee
Lee PR

Geek Tweet

The simplest form of online talk is the microblog (think Twitter). A microblog differs from a traditional blog in that its content is typically much smaller (in the case of Twitter tweets, 140 characters or less). Other leading social networking sites, such as Facebook and LinkedIn, also support microblogging in the form of status updates. As with traditional blogging, microbloggers post an unfathomable spectrum of content ranging from simple (and not infrequently inane) posts of the "What I'm doing right now" variety to deeper, to more thematic topics of interest to the author and their followers.

Although short in words, microblogging can be a powerful source of influence, engagement, networking, relationship building, traffic generation, and buzz. The trick is to simply be consistently active, authentic, knowledgeable, interesting, and responsive. Not as easy as it sounds, but many who have mastered the rhythms of this form of online discourse find that their authority, respect, and credibility within their online communities increases reliably over the course of time.

As noted in Chapter 1, microblogging has not been widely adopted within most geek communities as yet, which leaves quite an open field of opportunity for those that do. Some may look at the modest pace of adoption as evidence that geeks are inherently disinclined to use or value the potential of microblogging. Only time will tell, but several studies (most notably by Harvard Business School and Sysomos) that have tried to analyze the usage behavior of microblogging services have found that small groups of active users typically contribute to most of the activity. One example: in a 2009 Sysomos' Inside Twitter survey, based on more than 11 million users, shows that 5 percent of Twitter users account for 75 percent of all activity.[23] When weighing whether or not microblogging is right for your company, don't forget to consider that question from the other side of the equation by asking "What messages will our customers find relevant and interesting?" Unless your tweets are useful to them or you are building valuable relationships through friendly discourse, you might as well be talking to an empty room.

Start by understanding the conversations that are already happening online and then consider ways you'll be able to add value. Ask yourself: "Is this interesting or valuable from the customer's point of view?" If the answer is unclear, better to think that through than tweet with no purpose. You're representing your brand after all, so take whatever time is necessary to develop a crisp answer to that all-important question.

ConnectTweet

At Synopsys, we established a corporate Twitter account (http://twitter.com/synopsys), but rather than make one person exclusively responsible as the designated tweeter, we wanted to bring multiple Synopsys voices forward. Better that the "Voice of Synopsys" reflects the diversity of our company rather than unique personality of a single individual.

Given that the voices most likely to participate with the corporate Twitter account were already actively tweeting through their own personal accounts, we were initially concerned about the hassle of signing out of one account to log into another. Problem solved with an application called ConnectTweet (http://www.connecttweet.com). ConnectTweet enables designated users to stay logged into their personal Twitter accounts and, by adding add a hashtag (including a "#[topic]" to their tweets helps people searching for the "hashtag" topic) to their company-relevant tweets, the web-based application automatically scoops them up and posts them to the corporate account while still attributing them to the original tweeter. Thus, ConnectTweet allows a company's followers to clearly see the human voices on the inside.

"ConnectTweet is a simple utility built under the concept (reality in my opinion) that all groups, companies or brands are just collections of many people whose passion, ideas, and behavior completely shape it," said Ben Hedrington, the application's developer.[24] "Often those people's voices are drowned out in communications by a need to feel 'official' instead making it feel robotic, monochromatic and cold... this is especially evident as companies are showing up in social mediums like Twitter where forced news releases and push marketing stick out like a sore thumb...

"ConnectTweet flips that equation for groups and lets the real people all across your organization to show through on Twitter and be your voice. They can have real, human conversations with customers and share their unique perspectives and passion for their work as people at the front lines of your organization. This unique transparency shows the vibrancy that networks like Twitter have is inside your organization. It's just waiting to be shown the light of day."

Twitter Guidelines

To help our employees follow a common set of standards for content tweeted to the corporate Twitter account, we compiled the following guidelines:

- Be knowledgeable
- Be social
- Be relevant
- Avoid marketing hype, re-packaged news releases, and corporate-speak
- Do not become a spammer
- Respond to direct questions and comments
- When in doubt, escalate internally before posting externally
- Follow the corporate Social Media Policy
- Happy tweeting (and don't be a twit)

The savvy Twitter user realizes that effective communications aren't just pushing content to readers, but engaging in dialog. Unlike traditional forms of marketing, Twitter is "opt-in," meaning that users can "unfollow" other users with a simple mouse-click. For more interesting and valuable Twitter guidelines, check out Brian Oberkirch's "Advanced Twitter: Don't Tweet Like a n00b."[25]

The Art of the Retweet

Once you have a Twitter account, it's super-easy to interact by selectively promoting other people's content by "retweeting" their tweets to your own followers. Retweeting provides value to your social network by elevating content your followers might otherwise miss, plus it's a great way to express respect and build relationships with other content creators in your community.

To send a retweet, start by using the label "RT:" followed by credit to the originator with the syntax "@name" and completed with the original message. If there's room, the retweet can be made more valuable with a few words about what the original tweet is about or why you like it. Here is a full example:

> RT: @name http://bit.ly/ebiNLI—quality trumps quantity, even on Twitter

A note of caution is called for here: If the only content you provide through Twitter is to retweet other people's items of interest, that quickly becomes evident, putting you at risk of building a reputation of having nothing original to add to the conversation. Make sure to keep a balance between your own tweets and your re-tweets.

Online Forums

Twitter is broad but often fleeting—as tweets move through a timeline, inexorably replaced by newer tweets, they can be hard to access at a later date. Online forums, on the other hand, are topic-specific and built to be easily scanned. Forums provide discussion sites where people can hold "threaded" conversations, meaning that messages on the same topic are grouped together for easy reading. Such messages may or may not need to be approved by a moderator before they become visible, depending on the administrative preferences set up by the host.

Forums can provide tremendous value to technical communities based on the collective wisdom of their participants. As a knowledge base, a forum can hold answers to technical issues experienced by others for the benefit of everyone in the community. As such, establishing and maintaining robust online forums should be considered a high priority for any geek organization serious about supporting and interacting online with their user community.

Here are some tips on launching an online forum:

1. Pick a topic—the more specific and narrowly focused the better
2. Choose a forum platform that's visitor-friendly and easy to navigate

3. Set the ground rules (e.g., no spam, no rude behavior) and enforce them
4. Recruit a knowledgeable and engaged moderator. It's tough to build critical mass if it appears to forum visitors that the moderator is MIA or there's nobody home
5. Reach out to other experts on your forum topic and explicitly invite their participation. Exchange links. Comment on related forums. Engage
6. Create a community atmosphere and sense of belonging through engagement and interaction
7. Find ways to recognize and elevate active contributors
8. Make your forum content as attractive as possible to search engines
9. Just like everything else social media, honesty, trust, and respect are essential values for building a successful forum
10. Include a disclaimer. An example of one can be found on the Wikipedia site at:
http://en.wikipedia.org/wiki/Wikipedia:General_disclaimer

Knights of the Round Table

As you interact with your community online, always remember that you're participating in conversations that you don't dictate or control. Credibility and respect are earned, not awarded automatically just because you're speaking on behalf of a corporate brand. In developing your pattern of engagement, communication style, and place in the community, you could do worse than keeping King Arthur and his legendary round table in mind. As the name suggests, with no head of the table to be fought over, all who sat at it were ascribed equal value and stature. (That is, until they opened their mouths.)

Chapter 8

Host

Beyond listening, talking, and interacting, there's another powerful component to the social media mix: hosting. A function with many forms, hosting builds community in the physical and online worlds through acts of engagement in both. For those whose primary focus involves geeks and their particular slant on what makes for a good party, it can be one of the most valuable ways to show up in the world of social media.

Think Dinner Party

At its heart, hosting is an orientation to one's position in a group of people, a frame of mind. To host is to provide a comfortable environment in which people are invited to engage and interact. Virtually speaking, if your community website, technical forum, virtual tradeshow, or user group bulletin board provides the best coffee break in town, people will stop by and the word will spread. It's not because of your fabulous marketing slogans or best-in-class web design, but because a well-hosted environment can evolve into a rallying point for like-minded people to find each other, hang out, and talk shop.

To be an effective host, your job isn't to control the conversation; rather, it's to put on a good pot of coffee and make sure the room isn't too hot. Gracious hosts are adept at putting other people forward rather than hogging the spotlight for themselves. They stimulate interaction without dominating the conversation and often serve as a type of match-maker between parties they suspect might enjoy each other's company. They stay attuned to the ever-changing dynamics in the room and know when things need to be livened up a bit, or toned down to allow a welcome shift in energy. Your job as an online host is no different.

Elevating Others

Bloggers are often at their best when they think like hosts, inviting discourse by asking questions, linking to useful resources, and giving visibility and credit to others. The simple question "What do you think?" can be a great way to start an open-ended conversation. Commenting on and citing (linking to) content posted by others—particularly other bloggers in one's area of expertise—not only stimulates conversation, but is also one of the smartest things one can do to increase search engine visibility (more on that in Chapter 10).

In addition, bloggers have two highly effective methods at their disposal for putting other people forward: the guest blog and its close cousin, the written interview.

The New Geek Water Coolers

Engineers are a varied lot, spanning the gamut from Asperger's introverts to enthusiastic extroverts—the former are usually in charge of R&D and the latter the Marketing department. One thing they all have in common is that engineers will always prefer to consult, kvetch, and kid around with other engineers. Social media have a great future within the engineering community because they enable engineers to form communities with shared interests.

Aside from being the most effective way to hit the panic button if you get laid off, LinkedIn is a great way to stay connected with old colleagues and find out what it's like to work for a potential employer. LinkedIn groups are an excellent way to get help from others working on the same technical problems that are plaguing you. Expect this to happen more and more.

A lot of companies are using Facebook to put a human face on the corporation, but I think most engineers use it mainly to stay in touch with family and friends—I certainly do. Still, it's hard to have it both ways: presenting both a business face and a personal face at the same time. However, Facebook works well when you become friends with colleagues, so I expect engineers will increasingly take it up as they expand their social circles.

Twitter is another matter. Engineers have been slow to pick up on it. That's changing, since Twitter can quickly point you to a lot of technical material that you might otherwise have missed. Twitter is also a great way to follow people who usually have something to say that you'd like to hear. Still, Twitter is a bit "out there" for most engineers, so it may be a while before it hits an inflection point with them.

John Donovan
Editor/Publisher
Low-Power Design (http://www.low-powerdesign.com)

Guest Bloggers

Guest blogs provide a win-win for all concerned. For the host, featuring a guest blogger can help ease the burden of creating new content single-handed. For the guest, authoring original content for an established blog is a great way to communicate with people you might otherwise not be reaching. For the community, the value of the conversation is advanced through access to multiple expert voices. And, while hosting a guest blogger doesn't give you a total break from your blog responsibilities, it can bring a shift in engagement that's refreshing for you, the guest blogger, and your readers.

While it's possible to make an open "cattle call" for guest bloggers, we recommend that you hand-pick people in your geek world already known for their technical expertise *and* willingness to discuss their perspectives in a public forum. Where do you find these people? An obvious starting spot is to consider a sage co-worker in your department whom you know is respected in the greater outdoors, but who doesn't currently have a blog of their own. Remember, in the geek universe, the smart guys on the outside of your company are always looking for a way to "talk" to the smart guys on the inside. And while those inside smart guys may not be willing (or have the permission, or interest, or long-term commitment) to blog regularly, they might jump at the opportunity for a one-time gig.

Another obvious source for potential guest bloggers: people outside your organization who are already blogging on your topic. There are also other hiding spots where you may unearth a great candidate for a slot. Have you attended a conference lately and been impressed by a dynamic speaker or panelist discussing your topic? These folks have already demonstrated an interest in having their perspectives aired in public and might be open to the opportunity to share their insights with your readers as well. Have you read an actual book on your topic lately? Authors *love* the opportunity for a bit of free press and the chance to let your readers know they (and their book!) exist.

Assuming you've identified a warm body or two who would be a perfect fit to rotate into your editorial calendar, what do you need to keep in mind to make sure the experience is one you'll both want to repeat down the road?

Here are six things to consider when inviting a guest blogger to your blog:

1. *Make your expectations clear in your "Ask" message*
   Introduce yourself, your role, and the opportunity at hand. Provide links to help them quickly find your blog home page, adding links to any particularly relevant posts that will stimulate their interest in participating. This will give them an easy way to answer the inevitable question, "So, who is this person anyway?" In the initial email overture, we find it's best to just inquire about whether or not they would be interested in considering the opportunity, based on the simple specifications of a rough word count and the topic of your blog. There will be plenty of time to provide more detail after you've agreed to collaborate.

2. *Guide their choice of topic*
   If the potential guest responds in the positive, ask them to suggest a couple different angles they might like to take on their subject, being sure to "offer" (read: "insist") that you will be happy to help steer them to the one that will have the most appeal to your specific readership. Don't expect them to do the digging to find out what angles have been covered lately, and for heaven's sake, don't let them slog away at a topic only to have to come back after they submit their draft with an "Um... sorry, but we dealt in detail with ABC just last month. I was actually hoping you would cover XYZ."

3. *Align expectations: Agree on a deadline*
   Once you've agreed on a topic, you should also agree to a deadline. You may feel hesitant at first to set deadlines because, chances are, you aren't paying guest bloggers and most of them will have a paying day job. But the reality is that most people really do need deadlines to get stuff done, plus it helps you plan your editorial calendar.

4. *Reserve the right to edit*
   Even though the byline will be theirs, the typos or incorrect word usage will be on *your* blog if left uncorrected. While most guest bloggers will be grateful if you correct a typo, editing and changing phrasing (and therefore their "voice") may not be so welcome. When in doubt, it's best to err on the side of under-editing guest posts, but do try to work with the writer so the post is something

you're both happy with. It's a simple matter to email the blogger with your proposed edits and explain your rationale behind the revisions.

5. *Give credit where credit is due*
   Title all guest posts as such, and include the blogger's name at the top of the post. (Note: your blogging platform may still insist on listing you as the writer if you edited/posted the piece, in which case it's even *more* important to clearly identify the actual author.) Ask the guest blogger for a bio line complete with blog and website URLs, Twitter handles, etc., so your readers can follow them beyond your blog.

6. *Distribute the link*
   Within the first couple of email messages, let your guest blogger know when they should expect to see their post, then send out the link once it's live. This gives you a chance to thank them for their effort. Often guest bloggers will forward the link to their friends, post it on their own blog, or spread the word via Twitter.

See? Win, win, and win.

The Art of the Online Interview

Interviews provide another scenario where everybody wins. The credibility of the host increases proportionally with the quality of the topic and stature of the guest, and the interviewee can count on reaching new people beyond their existing sphere. Most of all, readers generally appreciate the availability of diverse insights and perspectives on the topics they're interested in following. The interview format is ideal for delivering high-value content that makes everybody happy.

A word of a caution here: Unless you are committed to starting and maintaining a blog that will be populated exclusively by interview posts, it's possible to overuse the approach. It's much better to mix-and-match interviews with your own voice, thoughts, research, and links. Otherwise, you may run the risk of being pegged as an "interviewer" rather than a blogger, which is fine if that's what you want to build as your online reputation. However, chances are that unless you're a Barbara Walters wanna-be, you'll want to intersperse interviews with other types of posts to maintain your credibility as an original(ish) thinker, not to mention someone other people might want to interview someday.

So how does one go about successfully developing and presenting such content? The process is very much like that described above for incorporating guest bloggers, but with a bit more work involved on your end.

Cold Calling: The "Ask via Email"

- Begin by introducing yourself. Include links to your company website and your blog.

- Set clear expectations for how the interview will be conducted and used. Provide a very brief outline of what you're up to, where it will be published, and when.

- Describe the interview process. Explain that once an interviewee agrees to participate in the online interview, the basic process consists of the following three steps:

    - You propose a set of interview questions and send them to the interviewee via email

    - They respond to the questions and send the responses back to you via email

    - You edit for typos, format, and publish the final interview as agreed.

- Provide the interviewee with clear information about how to contact you, and wait for them to say "Yes! I'd love to!" (The good news is that they almost all say "yes!") BTW, it really doesn't make sense to put more energy into the steps that follow until you've heard "yes." While it's not as heavy as writing a blog post from a cold start, your part of the effort takes a significant amount of lift, so don't begin until you know you'll get a decent return on your investment.

Preparation

- Once you've heard "yes" from the interviewee, begin your end of the deal by asking yourself: "What's the purpose of this interview?" Your answer to that question will help guide and inform the types of questions you ask.

- Prepare "topic buckets" for your questions. This will take some homework, but asking questions around topics that you already know your interviewee has an interest in or perhaps holds a controversial view on will both boost their enthusiasm for participating and will ultimately create more interesting content for your blog. The online research involved isn't strenuous, especially compared with the quality of the end result you can garner based on setting the correct trajectory from the front end.

- Structure the interview with a set of four to five questions (more than that can be burdensome, fewer can make for too short an interview).

- Think in terms of "What," "Why," and "How" to develop the interview questions.

- Questions should be phrased in an open-ended manner whenever possible (rather than ones that invite a "yes" or "no" answer).

- The primary purpose of your initial interview questions is to set the stage and provide easy openings for the interviewee to expand on the overall topic of the interview. If any of the proposed questions are off topic or awkward in any way, let the interviewee know that you are willing to edit the proposed questions—or ask different questions—if he or she prefers.

- Encourage the interviewee to provide URL links to sources for additional information, if appropriate. Remember, the whole goal of this effort is to provide opportunities to expand the community base, host a broader set of interactions, and create deeper connections to like-minded people and content. Even if the interviewee doesn't provide relevant links, do it yourself!

- Ask for any supplemental content you may need (e.g., photographs, illustrations) at the time you send the interview questions.

- The last question should encourage the respondent to provide any additional insights or information they wish to add, and is one of the most important questions on the planet, on any subject, ever: "Is there anything else my readers should know?" or "Is there anything else you'd like to add?"

Execution

- If you are confused or unclear by any of the responses you receive, ask for clarification.

- Trust and integrity are essential: If the interviewee requests that you consider any portion of the content provided as "off the record," always honor such requests.

- Check any linked URLs for accuracy before publishing.

- If any statistics are quoted or superlative claims made (XYZ is the most popular brand of widgets), make sure the source it cited.

- Format photographs, illustrations, and other graphic files as necessary to fit the parameters of your site.

- Ensure that contributions square with your company's social media policy. Although an interviewee from outside your company isn't bound by your social media policy in other places, the policy always applies to anything posted on your company's site.

- Proofread all content once again after formatting and before hitting the "Publish" button.

- Provide the interviewee with a link to the post once it's live.

- Remember to thank them for their time and thoughtful insights.

- Finally, and possibly most importantly, stay tuned to the post! Some of the most vigorous commenting back and forth on the blog Rick founded at Synopsys (*The Listening Post*[26]) happened as a result of an interview with John Donovan and some stimulating comments he made. By staying on top of the back-and-forth, Rick was able to participate through his own comments while simultaneously introducing himself to the other commenters, one of whom turned into a great interview subject himself (John Reardon).

One additional task that's ongoing in nature but that will serve you very well if you plan to host multiple interviews in the course of a year: Keep a hot-sheet of potential interviewees and what made you think they'd be good subjects at the time. It's simply amazing how blank a mind can go when you sit down to a blinking cursor with the intention of filling up the old blog pipeline but can't remember a darn person you thought just last week would make for a great interview subject. If you are blogging, you need to think, and act, like a writer. Keep that jot pad close to the bedside stand, 'cause baby, you're gonna need it!

Live Broadcast and Recorded Podcasts

Building on the power of the online interview, Synopsys launched a concept in 2009 called "Conversation Central." The original idea was to host a series of interactive discussions with industry leaders in a kitchen table-style chat room located at Synopsys' main exhibit booth at the Design Automation Conference (DAC) trade show.

The conversations, which were open to all DAC attendees to observe and/or participate in, explored topics such as how social media is changing the media landscape, influencing the employment market, and impacting competitive practices in cyberspace. When all was said and done, Synopsys had hosted 27 interactive sessions over the course of three days, inspiring one journalist to suggest that Conversation Central was "arguably the highlight" of the entire trade show.

One year later, Synopsys raised the bar for Conversation Central by broadcasting the live sessions over the web from the trade show floor at DAC 2010. The live broadcasts were enabled through BlogTalkRadio, a social radio network provider that enables anyone, anywhere to host a live, Internet talk radio show by using a telephone and a computer.

Similar to the previous year, Conversation Central engaged the participation—and, more significant, the imagination—of the surrounding community. But unlike the previous year, Synopsys left the Design Automation Conference with the newfound ability to broadcast interesting conversations and technically content-rich radio shows around the world, independent of a trade show or any other physical event.

Synopsys used that ability to immediately launch an ongoing series of Conversation Central radio shows. Hosted on the company's corporate web site, the Conversation Central program provides a good example of how acting as a host and putting other people forward can strengthen the success of the underlying social media program that put all the pieces together.

People Who Need People

Conversation Central evolved from a one-time physical event at a trade show to an online radio program that will live well into the future as a podcast available through its online archives. Moving in the other direction, community engagement also migrates from the online world into the physical one. One example is the Tweetup, which is a gathering of users brought together with Twitter. At conferences, for example, Twitter is increasingly used by attendees to arrange to meet during or after the event for discussion and face-to-face interaction.

From hosting an online interview to no-host bars, the common denominators are always the same: people, community, engagement, interaction. Think like a host, and you'll always be welcome at the party.

Social Media—Nein Danke?

According to Marcel Weiss, editor of one of Germany's most popular blogs, Germany is at least five years behind the U.S. when it comes to social media adoption, particularly with regard to blogs. Are my fellow countrymen really that closed to new ideas? Is there really an old and a new Europe? In "new Europe," Twitter helped organize social protesters in Moldova. Does it have to do with age?

I have been fortunate in being able to travel for business internationally and have noticed certain cultural differences along the way. In the US, for example, it's always easy to make initial contact. People often give me their contact information after a brief airplane ride, parting with the words "Let's have lunch" or "Give me a call next time you're in town, and we'll have a barbecue." They're surprised when I actually call.

In Germany, it is much more difficult to get over the initial hump of getting to know each other. Even the German language makes a distinction between "Du" and "Sie," the private and formal versions of the word "you." Once you know each other closely enough to arrive at "Du," there is no surprise when one actually calls.

The answer may perhaps lie in localization of social media. I get invites from German business associates to join them on Xing, the business network being more adopted than LinkedIn in Germany.[27] I keep a largely unmaintained Xing profile to connect but secretly hope that LinkedIn acquires them soon. Cultural differences become obvious almost immediately. On Xing, you better wear a tie in your profile photo. On LinkedIn people look much more casual.

On the private social media side, Facebook did not overtake its German competitor Wer-Kennt-Wen (translating as "Who Knows Whom") until late 2009. Localization probably is the answer here too, using the local language, and addressing some of the local cultural issues and concerns about privacy and security. A good example of privacy concerns is the strong opposition among Germans to technologies like Google Street View.[28]

Ultimately one sign gives me sure hope that things will change. The younger generation is all over Wer-Kennt-Wen and also tweets away on Twitter. But even my Dad—coming at this point with more than seven decades of wisdom—has a Facebook profile and eagerly follows updates of my wife, my 5-year old daughter's nanny, and me. Of course Facebook sends me concerned messages, inviting me to suggest more friends for him to increase his small network of three. I'll let him be but am quite proud that I seem to come from a family of early adopters after all.

Frank Schirrmeister
Director, Product Marketing and Synopsys blogger
A View from the Top—A System-Level Blog[29]

Chapter 9
Measure

Metrics are to marketing as statistics are to baseball, vital signs are to health care, or diagnostics are to tuning a car.

Measurement is widely regarded as an essential barometer of how well any given marketing initiative is working and, since the beginning of the marketing age, marketers have pursued reliable metrics as a cornerstone of responsible planning and decision making.

For those who salivate over the power of metrics, the online environment is a dream come true. Never before has it been possible to harvest so many details with such vivid granularity as with web analytics. In terms of "things that are trackable in marketing efforts," it's like going from the black-and-white first half hour of "The Wizard of Oz" to the Technicolor moment when Dorothy opens the door to Munchkin land.

But you're not Dorothy, and this isn't Oz, and having a customer click the mouse three times doesn't necessarily get you all the way home to Kansas.

As wonderful and powerful as web analytics are with the ability to track every mouse click on a website, the metrics they produce can only tell part of the story (so far). Marketing is part art and part science, and the scientist in every marketer (especially geek marketers) yearns for the ability to conclusively determine "If I do A, then B will always result." Web analytics can tell you a lot, but they can't do that.

Still, there's a rich treasure trove of what web analytics *can* do. The place to start is to clarify what you want to accomplish, and why.

Why Measure?

If Glinda the Good Witch of Web Analytics appeared in your office one day offering to help measure the success of your social media program, what three wishes would you ask for? Of everything that can be measured, what would you most like to know about the health and vitality of your program?

Page loads, unique visitors, returning versus new visitors? How about "What content is most popular?" or "How much time are people spending on my site?" What about the response rate to ads, white paper downloads, and other calls to action? Or lead generation leading (hopefully) to lead conversion? Or products sold and revenue generated? Careful with that last one—even Glinda has limitations. Unless your website is your one and only sales channel, mouse clicks are but one ingredient in a complex mixture of touch points leading to closing a sale.

It's important to know why you're measuring something—be it a social media program or the size of a room—so you'll know what to do with the information once you've measured. That may sound obvious, but sometimes the obvious stuff can be easily overlooked. Failure to understand why you're doing something can result in spending too much time on the wrong things, and worse, not enough time on the right ones.

Think about this: If your social media program doesn't produce X in measurable results by Y date, are you prepared to pull the plug on the program? Too extreme? How about this: "We're going to generate web metrics because that's just how we roll—we measure everything even if we have no idea how to use the results." It happens.

Taking the time from the outset to think through the "Why measure?" question will provide valuable context, ensure that you're measuring the right things, and save your team the busy work of producing reports that may never be used so they can apply their energies to more productive activities in other areas.

The complementary question "What will you do with the statistic?" can be equally informative. What action will you take based on answer X or Y? If you can't answer, you should think hard about the value of heading down that road at all.

What to Measure?

To quote a remarkable and revered geek from the nineteenth century, Lord Kelvin is credited with saying "To measure is to know" and "If you cannot measure it, you cannot improve it." Lord Kelvin also said that "when you can measure what you are speaking about, and express it in numbers, you know something about it; but when you cannot measure it, when you cannot express it in numbers, your knowledge is of a meager and unsatisfactory kind." Geeks love Lord Kelvin, and Lord Kelvin would have loved web analytics.

So, pretend for a moment that you aren't a social media program manager standing in front of Glinda the Good Witch of Web Analytics with your palms all sweaty as they hold your limp list of the three ROI questions you just know *someone* will demand of you tomorrow. Instead, now you're standing before the All Knowing and Powerful Lord Kelvin of Oz. What should you measure?

For Synopsys blogs, we've found it useful to measure, analyze, and distribute internal reports on the following:

- Visits (page loads)
- Unique visitors
- Page views
- Average time on site
- Returning visitors
- New visits
- # of RSS subscriptions
- # of new blog posts
- # of comments
- # of countries
- Top countries
- Top content
- Top referring sites

We believe that this set of key performance indicators (KPIs) provides insight into the health and vitality of our blogs and are helpful in understanding the level of interest and engagement the blogs are generating in the community. We also measure trends for each of the KPI values to observe progress through time.

There are multiple tools available to help compile most of the KPIs in the list above. The most popular free web analytics tool providers are Google Analytics and StatCounter; subscription-based tools are offered by Omniture Site Catalyst, Webtrends, and Coremetrics, among others.

Google Analytics

Synopsys uses Google Analytics to provide blog metrics. The primary reason why we measure is to help understand the value our social media program brings to the community (as measured by the KPIs specific to the community segment of the corporate website), so the program can be improved through time. Google Analytics is robust, it's free, and it maps directly to what we need to know to pursue those improvements.

Setting up a Google Analytics account is easy and begins at http://www.google.com/analytics. When your account is opened, you provide the URL for the website you want to track and Google provides a snippet of JavaScript code that you paste into your site. Where and how this is done—and what to do next—is the subject of numerous entire books, so it won't be covered here. The important thing to know from a social media planning perspective is that the snippet of code is the ticket to a cornucopia of data—and potential insight.

Those insights are harvested through a series of reports, the most useful of which include:

Visitor Overview:

A summary of how many new and returning visitors came to your site and how extensively they interacted with your content. This traffic overview allows you to drill down into aspects of visit characteristics (e.g., first time visitors, returning visits) and quality (e.g., average page views, time on site, bounce rate).

New vs. Returning Visits:

A high number of new visitors suggests that you're succeeding at driving traffic to your site, while a high number of return visitors suggests that the site content is engaging enough to keep 'em coming back.

Loyalty:

A high number of multiple visits from the same people indicate good visitor retention, while a high number of new visitors indicate good word of mouth and/or effectiveness in getting found through search engines. Both are good, but given the goal of building community, the former is the one to focus on growing.

Average Pageviews:

Average pageviews are the number of pages a single visitor will view during one visit. As an indicator of visit quality, a high number suggests that visitors are interested in the content offered across your site and are finding enough value to continue digging. Either that or your mother has an unhealthy obsession with your work product and possibly still has your first grade drawings taped to the kitchen fridge.

Time on Site:

When you can see that visitors are spending a lot of time on your site, that's another good indicator of visit quality. But be aware that this metric can be misleading if a visitor simply leaves a browser window open even though they have moved on to something else (and are not actually viewing your site). Unfortunately, there's no way to know for sure.

Bounce Rate:

Another measure of visit quality, bounce rate is the percentage of single-page visits where the visitor left your site from the same page they entered. Generally, it is thought that the lower the number the better, because a high bounce rate can indicate that the visitor landed on your page only to think, "Um...not what I'm looking for," or that they were insufficiently inspired to click beyond the entry page before leaving to go somewhere else. However, a high bounce rate can also mean that the visitor had a very specific "something" they were looking for (and for geek communities, this will often come in the form of an "on target" answer to a well-defined technical question), got to your page, and found exactly what they were looking for, and left your site to immediately get back to the lab and implement your brilliantly-supplied solution. In this case, a single-page entry/exit is probably a great indicator that your satisfied reader will think of your site the next time they have a question and come back to their new "tried and true" resource center.

As you can tell, metrics can be fascinating and informative regarding trends, but there is still a lot of unknowable gray area involved in the analysis and interpretation process. While it can be tricky, measuring without acting on what you find is a waste of time.

I've Measured—Now What?

Measurement is but one step in an ongoing process that begins with deciding (and periodically refining) what to measure, progresses through the creation of reports needed to support meaningful analysis, and concludes with continuous improvement to the program.

With the ability to generate more than 100 types of reports, Google Analytics can produce an overwhelming amount of data that has the potential to obscure the forest with too many trees. In addition, the structure and format of the non-customizable report templates is unlikely to match the intent and style of how you want to share data within your organization.

No worries. It's easy enough to capture the data you need within Google Analytics, export it to the environment of your choice, and format the data from there. One option to consider: a single page "at-a-glance" view of the most important KPIs for each individual blog. Some copy and paste is involved, but the resulting snapshot can help those on your distribution list understand the most important data without a Master's degree in web analytics.

Analysis-Based Insights

The ultimate purpose of measurement and reporting is to enable those responsible for the success of the social media program to make the best decisions possible about how to continuously improve. Analytics tools do an amazing job of capturing data, but it's the analysis that follows that creates actionable intelligence.

Once a program is established and starts to develop a track record, data points become trends—and that's where productive analysis begins. This is where the relationship between the frequency of blog posts and reader engagement becomes measurably visible, and where you can start making data-based assessments about which blog topics stimulate the highest response from the community.

Dig in and really study the data and you can learn a lot. Compare the trend line of your RSS subscribers with that of the unique visitors to your blog (remember that people who follow your posts in an RSS reader are able to read your content without actually visiting your site). What does the number of new versus returning visitors say about "visitor loyalty" or the discoverability of your content by first-time visitors who only know you exist because they found you through organic search?

What's the geographic distribution of the individuals in your community who visit your site? How much time are they spending on your site? What web page did they come from immediately prior to entering your site, what was their entry page, and what was the last page on your site they viewed before leaving to go somewhere else?

The analysis of your analytics will yield just the kind of factual details that will enable you to begin tweaking the dials on your social media machine with purpose and meaning.

The ROI of Social Media

With the abundance of web metrics comes the inevitable question, "What's the ROI of social media?" Not that social media is a black hole that absorbs copious amounts of investment dollars. Rather, it's the type of question typically asked by people who are simply trying to understand social media from a "prove to me that this stuff works" perspective.

ROI (return on investment) is a measure of something gained or lost relative to an amount invested. In many financial markets, ROI is fairly simple to measure: If I put $1,000 into an investment that pays 5% interest, I would expect to achieve an ROI of $50.

But in the field of marketing, ROI often defies such "cause and effect" simplicity. If you pay $10,000 for an ad, run it once, and nothing measurable happens, can you conclude that advertising doesn't work? Or that nobody reads the publication? Or that you completely wasted a bunch of money? Of course not, and the main reason is that marketing is not a one-time, flash-in-the-pan event.

Marketing is the orchestration of a journey of exposures, interactions, and experiences that happen over time. Just as ads are conceived in campaigns acting in concert with other points of exposure (e.g., PR, seminars, trade shows, sales calls), social media is an increasingly important component that complements the rest of the mix.

Measuring the ROI of social media isn't about looking for a more granular level of accountability than what's expected from other marketing resources. The metrics that matter are in the realm of figuring out how to track progress towards long-term customer-centric goals such as:

- Building trust relationships
- Increased customer engagement
- Enhanced customer experience
- Rapid response to customer feedback

In the view of organizational communications guru and International Association of Business Communicators (IABC) Fellow, Shel Holtz, it's virtually impossible to determine exactly how much money accrues to the company's bottom line as a result of one communications program or another.[30]

> "Return on Investment, when raised in the board room, is the amount, expressed as a percentage, that's earned on a company's total capital," said Shel. "A series of precise mathematical formulae are used to calculate ROI.
>
> "Of course, it's common to talk about return on investment more casually. You invest time, money, and resources in an effort and want to know what you got out of it. It's easy to refer to the results of your effort as ROI.

"The thing is, I don't understand why we're so obsessed with needing to prove ROI. We don't. What we need to prove is that we have set objectives for our efforts that support business goals and that those efforts produced measurable results. That's the kind of reporting that earns management respect and support for investment in communication.

"It's also the approach IABC—the International Association of Business Communicators—has been taking for at least as long as I've been a member (since 1977). To assess excellence in communication, IABC wants to know what objectives you set and how you can prove you achieved them. Nowhere does the label 'ROI' appear in these criteria. Nowhere does it need to.

"So I'm not suggesting that we don't measure the impact of our (communications) efforts, nor am I suggesting that we can't prove that there's value produced for the resources invested. But for the sake of our own credibility, unless we can come up with the numbers that reflect the way management perceives it, we need to stop trying to claim that it's ROI."

To carry the point a step further, most communications programs, no matter how well conceived and executed, function in concert within a larger stage. That stage includes other essential touchpoints with the target audience (e.g., Sales, Support) as well as utterly unpredictable—and therefore unrepeatable—serendipity (e.g., the casual comment, an unsolicited referral).

To say with total certainty that any single touchpoint was the one that closed the sale, modified the behavior, or otherwise accomplished the objective is next to impossible. Tough to make a lofty ROI claim in that context.

"The ROI of social media is that your business will still exist in five years," said Erik Qualman, author of *Socialnomics: How Social Media Transforms the Way We Live and Do Business*. In the geek-to-geek world, that's probably a bit hyperbolic, but still worth thinking about.

Geeks in the Semiconductor Industry

...invented the tools that other geeks use to create sites and apps such as Facebook, Twitter, foursquare, and LinkedIn.

Yet in my experience as a marketer in their world, the vast majority of geeks in the former camp are not the most social of creatures to begin with and treat all but LinkedIn with fear, loathing, and a general sense of trepidation.

True: A few geeks I've worked with eventually dipped their toes into Twitter—but most of them later burst into my office demanding reasons as to why so many "twits" (as one of them referred to Twitter users) would follow them, and then silently (and insidiously) "unfollow" them once they "followed" them.

I blame the steep social media learning curve for geeks on their trusting natures. They're not marketers and few have agendas.

They do use social media, however, when doing so can help them get work done. They're most comfortable with forums, where they can connect with like-minded geeks—though most like to silently consume past conversations vs. create a new one.

Many also read blogs but very few will ever comment on a post. That drives those running blog programs bananas, but I don't think it's a matter of shyness. It's simply that geeks don't like blathering on when there isn't anything of substance to add.

And let's face it: Blogs on EDA are not the most controversial on the planet.

Geeks like to absorb and then get back to work. So perhaps traditional social media use cases don't apply. You have to sell social media to them in a way that makes sense to them—even if it doesn't make sense to you (if that makes sense!).

Tom Diederich
Online Community/Social Media Manager, Ninety Five 5
Founding Online Community Manager,
Cadence Design Systems

Chapter 10
Lead

To build a solid and well-respected social media program in the G2G world is to display leadership, if only because such programs are not yet the mainstream norm in the geek universe.

Leadership is fundamentally a process of social influence that inspires and guides others toward beneficial outcomes. Leaders have the ability to tap into the important conversations that are shaping the world in the early stages, and then help others see the way forward. Leaders are among the first to notice trends, connect the dots, and identify opportunities within their midst. Perhaps most important, leaders manifest the confidence and courage to step beyond that which constrains the mainstream to usher new possibilities into reality.

Jack Welch, former chairman and CEO of General Electric Co., said, "Good business leaders create a vision, articulate the vision, passionately own the vision, and relentlessly drive it to completion."[31] To lead one's organization to social media success is a good place to start.

Lead People to Your Content

Leadership can take many forms. If you're the person in charge of your company's social media program, leading others to your site is an essential skill. There are many ways to accomplish that goal, but the most important is to ensure that the content creators in your organization are producing and maintaining the very best content possible for your site. Content is king in cyberspace; without it, nothing you can do to lead people to your site will have any staying power.

But let's say you have that part completely figured out. Beyond engaging with your community as discussed in earlier chapters, what can one do to increase the discoverability of their great content? Until recently, the best thinking was that Search Engine Optimization (SEO) was at the heart of the matter. However, given Google's new "Google Instant" search enhancements that offer suggestions as you type in a search term, SEO soon may not have the importance in the quest for increased discoverability it once had. The instant feedback, based on predictions of what you might be looking for, allows searchers to stop typing as soon as they see what they need. In other words, the technology customizes each person's search experience, thereby making a "one size fits all" optimization impossible. However, this still does not take away the need for content developers to be smart and informed about which tags and keywords should be included in their content to make it more easily found.

SEO, then, is simply the process of improving the visibility of a website to search engines so that when people are searching for content of the type featured on your blogs and other web pages, your site will show up in the search results—the higher on the list the better.

Of course, not everyone can appear at the top of the list in organic search,[32] or even in the first several pages of search results. Search engines like Google use proprietary algorithms to determine search rankings. Although the specifics are a well-guarded secret, Google considers factors such as how long your site has been established, visitor volume, number of inbound links (and the quality of those referrers) to establish the value, credibility—and ultimately the rank—of your content.

Rather than think of SEO as a method for cracking the secret code in an effort to move up the ranks, it's most productive to view SEO as a process to help search engines know what your pages are about. This is accomplished by optimizing your site with the right "keywords" placed in the locations where search engines look to categorize your content.

Keywords are the words and phrases that your potential customers and others in your community are using to search the web for content of the type featured on your site. First identifying and then intelligently using the best keywords on your web pages should be the core mission of your SEO strategy.

The "best" keywords are the words and phrases that:

1. most accurately describe your content, and
2. people are actually searching for regularly through Google and other search engines, and
3. have the lowest levels of competition from other websites targeting the same keywords.

Note that a word like "News" is unlikely to be good keyword for your site. Even if a candidate word is totally on target with the first and second criteria above, what are your chances of ranking higher than CNN or the *New York Times* for "News" in a Google search? To be successful in fulfilling their goal (to help make your content discoverable through a high search engine ranking), keywords must meet all three of the criteria in the paragraph above. HubSpot, an SEO and inbound marketing software provider, offers a Keyword Grader that can help jumpstart the keyword discovery process (http://www.hubspot.com/).

Best Practices in Leading Others to Your Content

Once you've established your keywords, where and how you use them makes a difference in leading visitors to your site. Here are some practical tips to help search engines find your site:

Page Headers

Page headers are one of the most important elements to telling both a user and a search engine what a certain page is about. Include target keywords in your page headers whenever possible, ensure that they accurately reflect the content of the page, and keep them short and concise to get maximum weight from search engines. Headers are created in HTML through the "h1" attribute, expressed as <h1>Your Really Meaningful Page Header Here</h1>.

Page Titles

Page titles are displayed in search results as the most prominent piece of information available to searchers. Page titles should accurately reflect the content of the page, use target keywords, and be unique for each page on your site (not duplicated). Page titles should also be succinct. Seventy characters is the maximum length that will be shown in search engines.

URLs

Try to include keywords in your URL addresses whenever possible, as in:

> http://www.company.com/keyword

> (or)

> http://www.company.com/keyword1-keyword2

Be sure that whatever keywords you choose accurately reflect what the page is about; doing so can help search engines understand the content of the page and, because geeks are prone to notice details like URLs, it can help them too. Separate words with dashes (not under-scores or blank spaces) and avoid characters like "@" and "?" which can confuse search engines (as well as browsers).

Images

Search engines can't discern the visual content of images on your site (yet), but you can describe it for them with tags. Tagging key images can help search engines know more about your site and help you rank in an image search for your keywords. Similar to the guidelines above, make sure the keywords you select are relevant and descriptive of the image. Tags are created in HTML through the "alt" attribute, expressed as:

<img src="path/meaningful-filename.jpg" alt="keyword"/>

Keep in mind that search engines also look at image file names (similar to how they look at URLs), so naming an image IMG001.jpg would be a missed opportunity in the context of SEO.

Inbound Links

Search engines are universally impressed with inbound links, and why shouldn't they be? When other sites think enough of your content to link to it from their own sites, that's a pretty good endorsement. So, in the midst of refining keywords and following SEO best practices, don't forget to reach out and build community with other sites through reciprocal links.

So there, in a nutshell, are the basics. There's plenty more to know, and no shortage of books, online resources, and knowledgeable consultants to help. Plus, beyond the on-page SEO fundamentals described here that can improve organic (non-paid) search results, there are numerous other methods for driving traffic to websites, including online advertising, pay per-click (PPC), database mining, email marketing, and more. But before pushing too far into any of these realms, consider the following suggestions from Matt Cutts, head of the Web Spam division at Google:

- Don't worry about endlessly optimizing for SEO—time is better spent creating content

- Write often; you'll get more practice, and it will build authority. Once you conquer your niche, then you can grow

- Don't overdo it! Going overboard with on-page SEO can and will hurt you. "If you read it aloud, and it sounds stilted, you're overdoing it"[33]

Lead People inside Your Company to Social Media

A special form of leadership is realized through lending a helping hand to others. From taking time to patiently answer a question or to help define a conceptual framework for how to think about an issue, teaching is an important component of leadership. Many believe, as do we, that sharing knowledge, insights, and best practices is an obligation that should be readily accepted by those who are privileged enough to have something of value to share.

As you make progress with your social media program and goals, try to always keep an open door to others who are interested in learning. Try also to remember what it's like to not know an alt tag from a bounce rate, or for that matter, why it's important to view social media as a conversation with those in your marketplace more than a marketing channel to push highly polished corporate messages through.

Teaching can take many forms, from leading a workshop to helping a new blogger find their way around WordPress, to sharing your social media knowledge through an internal blog. Regardless of the channel or venue, teaching is a mindset—and holding the intention to teach is the first step to making an impact in the world beyond the sphere of any one individual.

Lead the Smart People Outside Your Company to the Smart Ones inside

Amid the practical tips and pointers presented throughout this book, it's important to remember that social media is not an abstraction. It's completely real in that it provides context and the means for real people to interact in real ways as never before.

Most corporate marketing initiatives are conceived and implemented as programs. While there is certainly a broad range of scope, duration and success factors for any given marketing program—an advertising campaign as compared to a trade show or an email marketing effort as examples—must have a distinguishable beginning and end.

It's different with Social media initiatives. Unlike products or programs or campaigns, social media initiatives are best conceived as wide open stretches of terra firma where all manner of life happens, interacts, and grows. Marketing people are so well-attuned and competent at executing finite programs with vigor and focus that it's understandable if some miss this distinction at first. But we believe it's essential to look beyond strategic plans and SEO and metrics to truly see what social media really offer: Real life and amazing people.

Geeks are particularly amazing. Through their imaginations, creativity, training, and skill, they can legitimately lay claim to forever changing the world as we know it. They're the community, and they're not an abstraction.

Support them. Help them. Bring them forward. Make it easy.

With goals like these in mind, your social media program is bound to go far.

Lead People into the Unknown

Putting it all together, it becomes clear that building a successful G2G social media program is a substantial undertaking that takes every aspect of leadership one can bring to bear, not the least of which are the abilities to:

- Lead without being in charge
- Build consensus among supporters and doubters alike
- Engage with integrity, authenticity, and openness
- Act with humility, elevating others and giving credit where it's due
- Think creatively, dare to innovate
- Exercise patience while staying focused on the vision
- Bring a sense of humor, because...Dang! We're working with people here

The combination of these qualities plus a solid plan for action are sure to lead your G2G social media program in the right direction—the rest, as they say, is for the community to decide.

Notes

[1] http://bit.ly/e00jsq
(http://www.porticus.org/bell/bellsystem_ads-1.html)

[2] http://dictionary.reference.com/browse/geek

[3] http://bit.ly/120xUp
(http://www.urbandictionary.com/define.php?term=geek, Dec. 9, 2010)

[4] http://www.wikipedia.org/

[5] http://bit.ly/cKMzdl
(http://www.forrester.com/rb/Research/rethinking_b2b_tech_marketing_mix_in_digital/q/id/56610/t/2)

[6] http://bit.ly/d9BJrK
(http://www.eetimes.com/electronics-blogs/pop-blog/4199325/Engineers-dont-like-Twitter)

[7] http://bit.ly/cc3HEv
(http://danielnenni.com/2010/08/29/mobile-2drive-semi-4ever/)

[8] http://bit.ly/ar4VVt
(http://dbesem.blogspot.com/2010/06/dbe-releases-results-of-social-media.html)

[9] In 2008, we attended a panel discussion where we thought we heard social media expert Sean O'Driscoll warn against becoming mesmerized and side-tracked by the latest "shiny dime." It turns out that term he actually used was "shiny

diamond," but we think "dime" is more apt in describing the imbalance that's possible when an infatuation with social media bells and whistles causes one to lose focus on business objectives.

[10] http://bit.ly/cKMzdl
(http://www.forrester.com/rb/Research/rethinking_b2b_tech_marketing_mix_in_digital/q/id/56610/t/2)

[11] Doran, George T. "There's a S.M.A.R.T. way to write management's goals and objectives." Management Review, Nov 1981, Volume 70 Issue 11.

[12] http://www.pcmag.com/article2/0,2817,2361820,00.asp

[13] http://en.wikipedia.org/wiki/Exabyte

[14] http://slidesha.re/djv4Uf
(http://www.slideshare.net/livextention/a-comparison-of-social-media-monitoring-tools-a-white-paper-from-freshminds-research)

[15] http://synopsysoc.org/magicbluesmoke/

[16] http://bit.ly/OeTE1
(http://www.uberceo.com/home/2009/6/23/its-official-fortune-100-ceos-are-social-media-slackers.html)

[17] http://bit.ly/3iFu0
(http://www.web-strategist.com/blog/2007/12/28/defining-the-term-community/)

[18] http://bit.ly/ggt4Uh
(http://moblogsmoproblems.blogspot.com/2006/10/how-do-you-define-community.html)

[19] http://redcouch.typepad.com/weblog/2007/12/what-is-a-commu.html

[20] http://synopsysoc.org/thestandardsgame/

[21] http://en.wikipedia.org/wiki/Microblogging

[22] http://www.antseyeview.com/90-9-1-principle/

[23] http://www.sysomos.com/insidetwitter

[24] http://bit.ly/hWIc6B
(http://buildcontext.com/blog/2009/connecttweet-company-twitter-group-business-combine-voices)

[25] http://bit.ly/11oVJR
(http://www.brianoberkirch.com/2007/08/29/advanced-twitter-dont-tweet-like-a-n00b/)

[26] http://synopsysoc.org/thelisteningpost/

[27] http://bit.ly/hfPqwv
(http://www.socialmediadelivered.com/2010/06/21/social-media-tendencies-around-the-world-germany/)

[28] http://bit.ly/9nK0hU
(http://www.google.com/hostednews/afp/article/ALeqM5h5h55tBTr1LFxFWc6gkE_2E6tPdw)

[29] http://www.synopsysoc.org/viewfromtop/

[30] http://bit.ly/6Uwq4L
(http://blog.holtz.com/index.php/the_roi_label_and_the_credibility_of_communications/)

[31] http://bit.ly/9xodnh
(http://www.hrworld.com/features/top-10-leadership-qualities-031908/)

[32] http://www.hubspot.com/organic-vs-paid-search/

[33] http://success.hubspot.com/content-library/Tag/optimization

Notes

Authors

About the Authors

By day, Rick Jamison is disguised as a mild-mannered corporate communications contractor. But at sundown, he reveals his real superpowers as author and cartoonist. Part illustrator, part subject clarifier, and part Big Business underbelly tickler, his words and cartoons enlighten, enliven, enrich, entertain—and, from time to time, even educate.

Kathy Schmidt Jamison is a blogger, photographer, and humorist. She is Director of Strategic Communications at Synopsys where she's privileged to work directly for and with one of the finest übergeeks on the planet, Chairman and CEO, Dr. Aart de Geus.

Synopsys Press

About Synopsys Press

Synopsys Press offers leading-edge educational publications written by industry experts for the business and technical communities associated with electronic product design. The Business Series offers concise, focused publications, such as *The Ten Commandments for Effective Standards* and *The Synopsys Journal*, a quarterly publication for management dedicated to covering the issues facing electronic system designers. The Technical Series publications provide immediately applicable information on technical topics for electronic system designers, with a special focus on proven industry-best practices to enable the mainstream design community to adopt leading-edge technology and methodology. The Technical Series includes the Verification Methodology Manual for Low Power (VMM-LP) and the FPGA-based Prototyping Methodology Manual (FPMM). A hallmark of both Series is the extensive peer review and input process, which leads to trusted, from-the-trenches information. Additional titles are nearing publication in both the Business and Technical series.

In addition to providing up-to-the-minute information for design professionals, Synopsys Press publications serve as textbooks for university courses, including those in the Synopsys University Program:
http://www.synopsys.com/Community/UniversityProgram

The Synopsys University program provides full undergraduate and graduate level curricula in electronic design. For more information about Synopsys Press, to contribute feedback on any of our publications, or to submit ideas, please navigate to:
http://www.synopsys.com/synopsys_press

www.ingramcontent.com/pod-product-compliance
Ingram Content Group UK Ltd.
Pitfield, Milton Keynes, MK11 3LW, UK
UKHW022214230426
12048UKWH00016BA/846